The Logic of Lawmaking

INTERPRETING AMERICAN POLITICS
Michael Nelson, *Series Editor*

THE LOGIC OF LAWMAKING

A Spatial Theory Approach

. . . . .

GERALD S. STROM

The Johns Hopkins University Press

Baltimore and London

©1990 The Johns Hopkins University Press
All rights Reserved
Printed in the United States of America

The Johns Hopkins University Press
701 West 40th Street
Baltimore, Maryland 21211
The Johns Hopkins Press Ltd., London

The paper used in this book meets the minimum requirements
of American National Standard for Information Sciences—
Permanence of Paper for Printed Library Materials,
ANSI Z39.48-1984.

Library of Congress Cataloging-in-Publication Data

Strom, Gerald Steven.
  The logic of lawmaking: a spatial theory approach/Gerald S. Strom.
    p.   cm.— (Interpreting American politics)
  Includes bibliographical references.
  ISBN 0-8018-3992-0 (alk. paper).—ISBN 0-8018-3994-7 (pbk.: alk. paper)
  1. Legislative bodies—Voting—Decision making—Mathematical models. 2. Social
choice—Mathematical models. I. Title. II. Series.
JF525.S75   1990
328.3'75'0151—dc20   89-46209 CIP

For my family

CONTENTS

■ ■ ■ ■ ■

FOREWORD

■ ■ ■ ■ ■

Gerald Strom's *The Logic of Lawmaking* is, to specialist and nonspecialist alike, an appealing book for (at least) two reasons.

First, the book is at one and the same time a sophisticated but not a technical presentation of an important approach to the study of legislatures, namely, the spatial theory of legislative decision making.

Spatial models of politics have become increasingly more prominent in the literature of political science since the late 1950s, when Anthony Downs published *An Economic Theory of Democracy* (1957) and Duncan Black published *The Theory of Committees and Elections* (1958). Since then, according to a recent review by the political scientist Keith Krehbiel, more than ten dozen works have appeared that apply spatial models to the study of legislative choice. During the 1980s and early 1990s, the academic literature on legislatures, as reflected in the leading journals of political science, increasingly has been weighted toward—if not dominated by—articles that extend, criticize, apply, and develop the spatial theory.

Just what is the spatial theory of legislative decision making? Curiously, no book has appeared—until now—to initiate the uninitiated. Gerald Strom has written such a book. At the same time, he has probed the frontiers of spatial theory with ideas and insights of his own. *The Logic of Lawmaking* is a model of creative synthesis, that is, a work that brings a fresh perspective to a large body of scholarly literature in a way that advances as well as consolidates our understanding.

Second, in addition to Strom's treatment of spatial theory, his book is appealing because of the promise of the theory itself. The study of legislatures, like the study of politics generally, has been profoundly influenced over the years by the infusion of insights from other academic disciplines. From law and history, political scientists have learned the importance of the institutional design and development of legislatures. Sociology heightened our appreciation of legislative norms and of group influences on legislative activity. Psychology sharpened our understanding of political attitudes and behavior and of the nonrational aspects of legislative politics. Even anthropology has recently weighed in with a fresh approach to "tribal" behavior within the legislature.

The spatial theory, like other contemporary "rational actor" theories of politics, borrows extensively from microeconomics. But the theory is, as Strom argues forcefully, highly political. Although uninterested in one longstanding concern of political science—namely, the origins and development of political preferences—the spatial theory is profoundly interested in another, which Strom describes as "why a given outcome occurred as a consequence of the rules of the decision-making process and the rational, self-interested behavior of the decision makers."

Advocates of microeconomic approaches to politics in general and of the spatial theory in particular sometimes are guilty of intellectual triumphalism: at last the right path to understanding has been found! The same has been true of their historically, sociologically, psychologically, anthropologically, and even their biologically oriented colleagues in political science. Philosophers of science will not be surprised when I declare that they are all wrong. At the same time, however, their approaches are all valuable. The spatial theory of legislatures, like other theories, contributes to understanding simply by offering a new way to think about a very familiar but very important subject.

—Michael Nelson

PREFACE

■   ■   ■   ■   ■

At a panel on the current state of legislative theory at the 1988 annual meeting of the American Political Science Association in Washington, D.C., one of the major discussion items was the alleged lack of "politics" in rational actor (or social choice) theory. According to this critique, rational actor theory, and in particular, the spatial model form that is of primary concern in this book, is a formal and highly abstract exercise in logic or mathematics which has nothing to do with how Congress or any other political institution actually operates. Further, it is charged that in order to make the mathematics tractable, the theory relies on arbitrary and unrealistic assumptions that so greatly oversimplify reality that they can tell us little or nothing about how real political actors and institutions operate.

I have always found this critique of spatial theory to be interesting in large part, I think, because I have never understood it. In particular, I never understood what the politics is which is supposedly missing from the theory. Certainly, the rational actor literature is largely devoid of the insider tales of intrigue and gossip on which journalistic accounts of politics often focus. Then again, the other literatures in political science also generally ignore such "data." The *American Political Science Review* and the other professional journals have never been known as a primary source of the latest Washington intrigues.

Alternatively, the lack-of-politics charge might refer to the lack of empirical data analysis in much of the spatial theory literature, and this would be partly true. Many of the books and articles that have contributed to the development of this theory do not analyze data and test empirical hypotheses. However, for two reasons it does not follow from this that the theory is nonempirical. First, from its inception, the developers of spatial theory have concentrated on trying to explain the politics of real political institutions and have sought empirical evidence for the hypotheses that follow from the theory (see in particular Riker 1958, 1965). Such efforts continue, as work by Shepsle and Weingast (1987) and many others indicates.

Second, in the development of a science, a certain amount of division of labor becomes necessary at some point whereby some people focus more on theoretical developments while others devote their attention to testing hypotheses derived from theory. This is certainly true of the rational actor literature in which, as noted above, many of the books and articles focus exclusively on the rigorous extensions of the basic theory (see, e.g., McKelvey 1986). Other articles focus upon either the experimental (e.g., Fiorina and Plott 1978; Wilson 1986) or empirical testing (e.g., Krehbiel 1987) of hypotheses derived from theory.

Another interpretation of the lack-of-politics charge, and the one I suspect is usually behind the criticism, is that rational actor theory does not attempt to explain a particular phenomenon in which someone is interested. For example, in the behavioral approach—the other major paradigm in legislative studies—the focus is primarily on explaining why political actors behave the way they do. The behavior of individual members on roll-call voting in Congress, for example, may be explained by such variables as party, ideology, or some other political or personal characteristic. Further, by focusing upon the behavior itself, such studies generally ignore the consequences of the behavior. They can explain why members of Congress voted the way they did but not why the resulting outcome took the form that it did—that is, why bills contain the provisions they do.

In contrast, rational actor theory, especially in the form taken by the spatial theory of decision making, does not place much emphasis on explaining the details of individual behavior. Instead, it focuses on explaining why a given outcome occurred as a consequence of the rules of the decision-making process and the rational, self-interested behavior of the decision makers. Thus, in this paradigm, the focus is on explaining outcomes and how these change with changes in either the rules of the political game or the preferences (or goals) of actors. In attempting to do this, it is hard to understand how spatial theory could be thought to lack politics.

The analysis reported in this book, along with an examination of the politics of spatial models, has two major purposes. First, it summarizes the spatial theory literature on legislative decision making and, at various points, attempts to contribute to this literature (e.g., by showing that rules that individually contribute to the stability of social choice outcomes can, in unison, interfere with each other's stability-inducing properties). Second, in presenting spatial theory in a largely nontechnical manner, the book hopefully makes the elements of the theory accessible to a wide range of students and legislative scholars.

While working on this manuscript, I benefited from the assistance of a number of people. I especially appreciate the comments, suggestions, and advice I received from Barry Rundquist, Mark Lichbach, Paul Quirk, John Williams, Richard Johnson, Ike Balbus, Michael Nelson, and a reader for the press. I also appreciate the assistance of Executive Editor Henry Tom, Marge Nelson, and my administrative assistant, Francine Cannarozzi.

The Logic of Lawmaking

INTRODUCTION

. . . . .

On September 25, 1986, the U.S. Congress passed and sent on to the president a five-year extension of federal programs for higher education. This large and very complicated bill (S 1965):

1. Authorized $10.2 billion for 1987, with more than half of this funding going to two student aid programs ($4.6 billion for Pell grants and $3.2 billion for guaranteed student loans)
2. Increased the amount students can borrow per year and more than doubled (from $25,000 to $54,750) the total amount a student could borrow
3. Allowed students, for the first time, to receive Pell grants if they were not enrolled as full-time students
4. Required all students to pass a financial needs test to qualify for loans
5. Required students to maintain a "C" average by the end of their sophomore year to continue to qualify for loans
6. Authorized $60 million for programs to recruit and train high school and elementary school teachers
7. Authorized $120 million to help colleges with financial difficulties to improve their programs and management
8. Reauthorized a program of loans to help colleges construct student housing.

This list includes just a few of the provisions included in this bill, but it gives an indication of the diversity of provisions this one bill contained. Some of these provisions set the aggregate spending levels for various programs, others spell out various requirements that must be met for students to receive financial aid, and still others are concerned with providing direct federal assistance to college and universities.

Despite the hundreds of different provisions included in the bill, however, not everything that different political actors wanted was included. For example, the bill did not make the $4 billion in cuts in higher education spending which the Reagan administration had proposed. Instead, the new authorization level for 1987 was $1.7 billion greater than the appropriations level for 1986. It also did not reverse the trend of more loans and fewer grants to lower income students which several organizations had proposed; and it did not include a provision, backed by Education Secretary William Bennett, that would gear repayment installments to after-graduation income. Instead, only a pilot project was included to test how such a program would work.

What happened as Congress considered the higher education bill is typical of what happens to most bills. Some provisions that people want get included, other provisions are not included, and still others are included in modified form. Why is this the case? Why are some included whereas others are not? Did the procedural rules under which the bill was considered have any impact on the outcome, and would a different set of rules have produced a different outcome? Moreover, before it actually passed, was there any way one could have anticipated (or predicted) which provisions would be included in the higher education bill and in what form?

One way of explaining why some provisions were included and others were excluded from the higher education bill is to focus on the specific events at various points in the congressional process. Thus, for example, the House bill retained provisions in existing law requiring students to pay a 5 percent fee when they first take out a loan because of a compromise between William Ford (Democrat, Michigan), the subcommittee chairman and chief sponsor of the bill, and E. Thomas Coleman (Republican, Mississippi), the ranking subcommittee Republican. During debate in the full House, Ford reportedly agreed to accept the 5 percent fee amendment offered by Coleman in return for an agreement that Coleman would not offer other cost-cutting amendments.[1] Other provisions could be explained in similar ways. Such explanations give us a sense of having explained what happened to each of the provisions of the bill and, *in toto*, what happened to the whole bill.[2] Such explanations also have an *ad hoc* character and tend to focus on the characteristics of particular individuals and the supposedly unique circumstances in which they find themselves. Because of this focus, they usually do not help us understand either what will happen the next time Congress considers a higher education bill, or what will happen to other bills that have nothing to do with higher education.

Ideally, one would like to be able to explain what happened on the higher education bill as an instance of some general or typical way legislatures like Congress operate. However, this would require a theory of legislative policy making to specify which characteristics of the legislative process cause particular preferences to be included, excluded, or modified. The problem in developing such a theory is that modern legislative processes like those in Congress are complex in at least two different ways. First, they are characterized by preference complexity. Many different people want many different provisions included or excluded from particular bills. Each of the 435 representatives and 100 senators may hold different views of what should and should not be included in any piece of legislation. In addition, there are thousands of lobbyists, members of the federal bureaucracy, the president, and state and local governmental officials, as well as ordinary citizens who are trying to influence the actions Congress will take. Any legislation that is passed will reflect some but not all of the preferences of these various actors, and a theory of legislatures needs to be able to explain why some preferences are included and others are excluded.

Second, modern legislatures are characterized by procedural complexity, reflected in both the numerous parliamentary rules under which they operate and in the multiple stages of the legislative process itself. In Congress, for example, most of the major legislation that is eventually enacted into law must journey through ten to fourteen separate steps: it must be introduced (1) in the House and (2) in the Senate; it must be considered and passed by (3) a subcommittee and (4) committee in the House as well as by (5) a subcommittee and (6) committee in the Senate; it must be considered (7) by the House rules committee; it must be voted on (8) in the full House and (9) full Senate; it might need to go through (10) a conference committee to resolve the differences between the House and Senate versions; which then requires that it once again pass (11) in the full House and (12) full Senate. Then it must be signed by the president (13) or, if vetoed (14), the veto must be overridden in both chambers of the Congress (15). Moreover, at each of these stages, there are different sets of procedural rules that both facilitate and constrain various kinds of actions. To explain the outcome of a legislative process, a theory

Table I.1. Selected Provisions of the Higher Education Act at Five Points in the Legislative Process

Provision	House Committee	Full House	Senate Committee	Full Senate	Conference
Aggregate authorization level	$11.1 billion	$10.7 billion	$9.7 billion	$9.5 billion	$10.2 billion
Guaranteed student loan					
For freshman and sophomores	$2500	$2500	$3000	$3000	$2625
For juniors and seniors	$5000	$5000	$4000	$4000	$4000

needs to be able to explain the impact of these various rules on outcomes.

As a very simplified illustration of what can occur to provisions of a bill traveling through this process in one Congress, consider Table I.1, which shows the outcomes at just five stages of two provisions of the higher education bill. First, consider the provisions regarding the total amount of federal spending for higher education in the 1987 fiscal year. As reported by the House Education and Labor Committee, the bill had a total authorization level of $11.1 billion, which was then reduced on the House floor to $10.7 billion (this was done by the committee accepting an amendment retaining the 5 percent fee that students pay when they take out a loan). In contrast, the Senate Labor and Public Welfare Committee reported the bill with aggregate spending of $9.7 billion, which was reduced on the floor to $9.5 billion (accomplished by acceptance of a set of amendments introduced by Majority Leader Dole, which cut the maximum amount for individual Pell grants and in special allowances for banks). Thus, the two committees reported bills with different spending levels, and the two full chambers reduced both these levels in different ways. The two bills then went to a conference committee to resolve the differences between the House version, which authorized $10.7 billion, and the Senate version, which authorized $9.5 billion. The conference compromised this difference with a slight advantage to the House, agreeing to a final authorization of $10.2 billion (which was $0.5 billion less than the full House amount and $0.7 billion greater than the full Senate amount).

Consider now the second set of provisions, those specifying the maximum amounts students could receive each year from the guaranteed student loan program. As Table I.1 shows, a different pattern exists here from that seen earlier on the authorization level. In the maximum loan case, both chambers agreed with their committee recommendations on these provisions, but the amounts on which the chambers agreed differed from each other. Accordingly, the conferees compromised on an amount for freshmen and sophomores closer to the House bill but accepted unchanged the Senate figure for juniors and seniors.

These examples of preference and institutional complexity illustrate a basic problem of understanding and predicting legislative policy making. Sometimes a committee member's preferences are included in committee bills, and sometimes they are not. Sometimes full chambers accept the recommendations of their committees, whereas at other times they modify (or even reject) them. Sometimes conference committees appear to favor the provisions in one chamber's version of a bill over those in the other. Explanations of why certain preferences will be added or dropped in these various settings are basically missing in the traditional literature on legislative policy making.[3] In addition, the effects on legislative outcomes which various parliamentary rules and legislative structures like committees have are not well understood.

These are questions that a theory of the legislative process should be able to answer if it is to be useful in explaining the policy outcomes produced by modern legislatures. The difficulty is that with both preference and procedural complexity, developing a realistic theory that allows explanation of policy outcomes is very difficult. However, as subsequent chapters will show, by making a series of simplifying assumptions, slow but steady progress has been made over the past several decades in developing a theory capable of predicting policy outcomes.

The legislative theory of concern here is the spatial theory of legislative policy making. The goal of this theory is to identify the interrelationships among the preferences of legislators, the strategies these legislators adopt for attaining these preferences, the legislative rules under which these strategic choices are made, and the final legislative outcomes that result. As described in Chapter 1, the theory is based on a number of simplifying assumptions about how legislative actors behave and the rules under which they operate. Based on such assumptions, this theory purports to identify those features of the legislative process that—if present in any particular policy-making process—allow one to predict the content of policy coming out of the process.

In doing this, it should be noted that the focus of the theory presented here is the internal workings of the legislative process. The main actors are legislators, the main motivating factors are the wants or preferences of these legislators, and the context in which they seek to attain their preferences is given by the rules and procedures of the legislative process. Excluded from consideration are such nonlegislative actors as voters, interest groups, and members of the bureaucracy. Although no one familiar with the legislative process in Congress would deny that such nonlegislative actors can often have a significant influence on both legislative processes and the policy outcomes of these processes, their influence in the theory presented here is assumed to operate by affecting the preferences of legislators. Thus, for example, an interest group will be influential to the extent to which it can persuade various legislators to pursue its policy goals.

How a group might do this, however, is not considered in the theory presented here, which takes as its starting point legislators holding a set of policy preferences.

The chapters that follow describe the basic spatial theory of legislatures and how this theory treats the problems of legislative policy making. The progression of chapters in part moves from the simple to the complex but also in part parallels the historical development of the theory. The latter is seen most clearly in the attempts of the theorists to come to grips with the fundamental problem of the spatial theory of legislatures, namely, that legislative decision making may be very chaotic and unpredictable. This is an especially important problem in that this prediction apparently contradicts the observations of generations of observers of real legislatures like the U.S. Congress. As will be seen, attempts to reconcile this apparent discrepancy between theory and observation have been a major factor in promoting the development of increasingly sophisticated spatial theories.

1

DEFINITIONS AND ASSUMPTIONS

■ ■ ■ ■ ■

This chapter introduces the basic terms and assumptions of the spatial theory of legislative decision making. These include assumptions about who the effective actors are in legislative decision making, how they decide among alternatives, and how their decisions can be represented in an analytical model.

The spatial theory of legislative decision making described here belongs to the large family of rational actor theories.[1] All these theories assume that people have wants or goals of various kinds and that they can generally be expected to act in ways they believe will lead to the attainment of them. As so stated, this is an assumption with which few would disagree, for experience and observation tell us that this is how we ourselves try to behave and how we expect other people to behave as well (and if they do not behave in this way, we think there is something strange about them). This does not mean, however, that people always get what they want. It may be physically or logically impossible for them to attain some of their goals, or they may lack relevant information about the options among which they are choosing, or they may fail to process the information efficiently or effectively they do have. Rationality, in other words, is not concerned with end results as such; it is concerned with the *process* by which individuals try to attain the goals they set for themselves. At times, one may think that someone is pursuing an unattainable or a morally objectionable goal (e.g., building more weapons at the expense of higher education programs). One may think that such people are misguided or ill informed, but they would be considered irrational only if their actions bore no relationship to the goal they had set.

Note, too, that rationality does not necessarily imply that people are selfish hedonists who care only about themselves. In rational actor theory, people's wants or goals are taken as given. How they pursue these goals is what the theory of rational action addresses. Altruists who wish to help others need to act as rationally to attain their wants as self-centered hedonists do in trying to attain their self-centered goals. Why people want what they do is not part of the theory of rational action, only how they go about trying to attain their wants is.

The Theory of Rational Action

In thinking about how rational actors can be expected to behave in various circumstances, scholars from disciplines like economics, psychology, political science, and others have developed an extensive theory of rational action. In developing this theory, the term *wants* as used above is usually replaced by the term *preference*, so it can be said that people have preferences and act to attain them.

What does it mean to act to attain one's preferences? To answer this question, a distinction needs to be made among four concepts: (1) preference; (2) outcome; (3) action; and (4) strategies. In rational actor theory, people are assumed to have *preferences* for *outcomes* and to formulate *strategies* for *actions* they believe best suited to bring about their preferred outcome. In legislatures, for example, the outcomes are bills, so it is assumed that legislators have preferences for bills and the provisions of bills. In turn, they formulate strategies of how to act (e.g., vote) to produce the bill that will give them the greatest amount of satisfaction. In this sense, preferences for outcomes are linked to actions like voting, proposing amendments, and making speeches by the strategies legislators adopt. These strategies define the appropriateness of their various actions for bringing about their preferred outcome. Thus, in a nutshell, rational legislators develop and implement strategies for action designed to bring about outcomes they prefer.

Saying that people develop strategies and act on the basis of their preferences for outcomes makes preferences the fundamental basis for behavior. Moreover, as the theory has been developed in the legislative context, the preferences of most concern are those for bills and the provisions of bills. Because of this, such things as party loyalties, loyalties to institutions like the House or Senate, and loyalties to the president are not accorded particular prominence. This is not because such loyalties do not exist. The voluminous literature on Congress suggests that not only do they exist but they are very important in determining how legislators behave.[2] How, then, can such factors be ignored, and will this not give a very distorted view of legislative decision making? Certainly, if one is interested in legislative parties or congressional-presidential relations, ignoring party or institutional loyalties is problematic. However, the rational actor theory described here is not intended to explain such things. Rather, it is intended to explain the *outcomes* of legislative decision making and how these outcomes are related to the preferences of legislative actors. Moreover, as already noted, this theory is not concerned with the origins of a legislator's preferences or why particular actors hold the preferences they do. In this sense, such things are party loyalty, loyalty to the president, and a desire to be reelected are sources of preferences or are reasons for various legislators holding the preferences they do, but this is outside the realm of the rational actor theory, which is concerned with the process by which rational actors pursue whatever preferences they decide to pursue.

As a criticism of the theory discussed here, it can also be argued that such things as party or presidential loyalties are more than a source of preferences for legislators. They can also provide behavioral cues such as how to vote on a particular bill.[3] In the terms used above, this is equivalent to providing strategies for action so that such loyalties provide a legislator with both preferences and strategies. Given the large number of very complex bills considered by a modern legislature, no legislator has the time or energy to examine both the content of all the bills considered and to develop maximizing strategies for making each of them conform as closely as possible to his or her preferences. Moreover, the information needed for such an effort would be very great and prohibitively expensive to acquire. Because of these limits, legislators cannot hope to develop comprehensive, maximizing strategies but must rely in large part on strategies like taking cues from party leaders or the president which, experience has shown them, will give them a satisfactory if not maximal amount of goal attainment.[4] Then, how can a rational actor theory be valid which presupposes that each legislator develops maximizing strategies for each bill?

Before addressing this criticism, a related criticism should also be noted. The rational actor theory discussed here presumes that legislators do not make mistakes in developing their strategies for action.

However, there is a large empirical literature suggesting that people frequently perceive information incorrectly or make errors in processing it and, as a consequence, cannot develop appropriate maximizing strategies for attaining their goals.[5]

At an empirical level, the rational actor theory presented here must acknowledge these criticisms as valid. At the theoretical level, however, both these criticisms are largely ignored and for good reasons. To include the possibility of mistakes in information perception or processing along with the possibilities of strategies for dealing with these difficulties would make developing a theory very difficult and the theory itself very complex. Moreover, the theory here is trying to describe the general or central tendency of legislative behavior and is willing, as the price paid for advancement, to ignore for the present factors that cause deviations from the central tendency. As an illustration from a different area of what is meant by this, consider a physicist asked to predict where a given leaf that falls from a tree will land. From the theory of gravity, the physicist knows that the leaf will generally fall downward (the central tendency) and probably not too far from the tree on which it grew. Yet, because of the uncertainties of wind direction and the likelihood of gusts of varying degrees of intensity, the physicist cannot predict precisely where a given leaf will land. Similarly, in developing the spatial-rational actor theory of legislative decision making, theorists have chosen to ignore wind gusts and focus primarily on the central tendency of legislative behavior as determined by the preferences of legislators and the errorless strategies they adopt to maximize the attainment of their preferences.

The Nature of Legislative Preferences

Once it is taken as given that legislative actors have preferences for legislative outcomes (regardless of the source of these preferences) and can adopt maximizing strategies to attain them, the next step is to examine the relationships among these given preferences. A core element of the rational actor theory is a set of assumptions about people's preferences. If you prefer both to read this book and not to read it, you have a problem because your preferences are contradictory. In such circumstances, it is impossible to act rationally to pursue your preferences because you cannot develop a strategy that simultaneously allows you to read and not read this book. Presumably, the fact that you got this far indicates that your preference for reading this book outweighs your preference for not reading it (of course, this might change as you proceed). Moreover, in continuing to read, you are giving up opportunities to do other things you might also prefer, like reading a different book, watching television, or going to a movie. What this example illustrates is that, at any given time, people have many different preferences, and these preferences are related to each other. It is these relationships among preferences which the assumptions discussed below concern.

If you were a member of the U.S. House of Representatives in 1986 and could choose between voting for or against the higher education bill as it emerged from committee, only one of three possible conditions logically must characterize your preferences for these two options. (1) You can prefer the bill to the status quo of no bill; (2) you can prefer the status quo to the bill; or (3) you can prefer them equally (in which case, you are said to be indifferent between the bill and the status quo.)[6] The fact that only one of these relations must hold between the two preferences is referred to as the *connectedness* axiom. In requiring connectedness, rational actor theories are requiring that an actor's preferences concerning a given set of outcomes are connected or related to each other so they can be compared. More technically, if we let $u(B)$ represent the amount of utility or satisfaction a person would receive if the bill passes and $u(Q)$ the amount of utility if no bill passes, then we can express the connectedness axiom as implying that only one of the following relations holds:

$$u(B) > u(Q)$$
$$u(B) < u(Q)$$
$$u(B) = u(Q)$$

Also, by letting P stand for *is preferred to*, the first of these relations could have been written BPQ; and by letting I represent *is indifferent to*, the last one could have been expressed as BIQ. Finally, the relation R is defined as *is preferred to or is indifferent to* and can be defined formally as either P or I. Using this new symbol, the connectedness axiom can be written as either BRQ or QRB. Expressions like $u(B)$ occur frequently in the literature of rational actor theory, and it is important to be clear about what such terms mean. Above, $u(B)$ was defined as *the utility that an actor associates with outcome B*. What does this mean? As used in rational actor theory, utility is an abstract concept. Utility itself is never observed, and there is no need to measure it precisely because there is no need to know just what value

$u(B)$ has.[7] Rather, all one needs to know is whether $u(B)$ is greater than, less than, or equal to the utility associated with some other outcome. That is, it is the *relationships* among the utilities associated with various outcomes which are important. One wants to know whether $u(B) > u(Q)$, or $u(B) < u(Q)$, or $u(B) = u(Q)$, not the precise values of $u(B)$ or $u(Q)$. All one needs to know, in other words, are ordinal relationships, not interval values.

Also note that as a consequence of the precise value of $u(B)$ being unobserved and unmeasured, there is no way one can compare the utility of two different actors. It can be said that two actors both prefer $u(B)$ to $u(Q)$, but one cannot say that one of them prefers B to Q more than the other one does.[8] Because such interpersonal comparisons of utility are not possible, the only utility comparisons made are for a single actor; and if many actors are involved in a decision, a separate set of comparisons is made for each person.

Now, consider a choice among three alternatives: a bill reported from a committee (B), an amended version of this bill (A), and no bill (or the status quo, Q). If a legislator prefers the bill over the amended version of the bill and prefers the amended version over no bill, should the legislator also prefer the bill over no bill? If so, this legislator would be said to have *transitive* preferences. Rational action presumes transitive preferences so that BPA and APQ implies BPQ.[9] Without it, a legislator cannot develop a strategy to pursue his or her preferences effectively. If the legislator prefers the bill to the amended version, the amended version to no bill, and no bill to the bill, his or her preferences are *intransitive*. Therefore, this legislator, with BPA, APQ, and QPB, cannot make a rational choice because regardless of what alternative he or she chooses, there will always be a better alternative available. Thus, if the legislator thought about voting for the bill, he or she would not because no bill is preferred; but the legislator would not vote against the bill either because the amended version is preferable to no bill; and finally, the legislator would not vote for the amended version because the bill is preferable to the amended version. Theories of rational action, through the transitivity assumption, assume that such vicious circles do not exist.[10]

These two assumptions or axioms, connectedness and transitivity, are the core of all theories of rational action. They imply that a rational actor has a consistent and noncontradictory set of preferences over any set of alternatives. It is thus assumed that the choices a rational actor makes as a consequence of these preferences will also be consistent. This consistency, in turn, implies that the behavior of a rational actor is predictable from a knowledge of his or her preferences.

Note, finally, that rational actor theory as described here assumes a relatively short time perspective within which actors do not change their preferences. Thus, the consistency referred to above is a short-term consistency resulting from a fixed set of preferences over a set of alternatives. This is consistent with the fact that rational actor theories take preferences as given and do not try to explain why people hold the preferences they do. Nothing in the assumptions, however, precludes rational actors from changing their preferences over time. All that is required here is that actors do not change their preferences while in the process of deciding among a particular set of alternatives. In other words, preferences are assumed to be fixed during the duration of a given decision-making process.

Representing Preferences

A useful way to examine and analyze preferences (and the behaviors they cause) is to represent them pictorially or spatially. One very useful way this can be done was suggested by Black (1958). On a two-dimensional graph, let the *horizontal axis* (the *abscissa*) represent outcomes on which actors have preferences, and let the *vertical axis* (the *ordinate*) represent their preference rankings. With the higher education bill, for example, the three options of no bill, reported bill, and amended bill can be represented along the horizontal axis, and the preference ranking of legislators for these alternatives can be represented on the vertical axis as in Figure 1.1. It does not matter (at this stage) in what order the alternatives are placed on the horizontal axis, nor is it presumed here that distance has any signif-

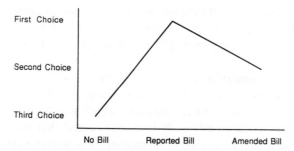

Figure 1.1.   Individual Preference Curve over Three Alternatives

icance on either axis. The preferences of a legislator who most preferred the reported bill can be represented by placing a dot at the point at which lines drawn from *reported bill* and *first choice* meet and similarly for the legislator's other preferences. If these points are now connected by a line, always moving from left to right (and knowing that the spaces between the alternatives are meaningless), a preference curve for this individual is created (as in Fig. 1.1).

Note that the ability to represent preferences in this way requires that these preferences be both connected and transitive. Connectedness implies that preferences over outcomes are related to each other and hence can be represented together on the same graph. Transitivity, in turn, actually allows one to place the points in the figure. To see this, consider what would happen if a legislator did not have transitive preferences. In the case illustrated in Figure 1.1, for example, if a legislator held the preference order no bill > amended bill > reported bill > no bill, which outcome is his or her first choice? It cannot be no bill because both the amended bill and the reported bill are preferred to no bill. Likewise, it cannot be either of these others because no bill is preferred to them. Thus, in representing preferences as in Figure 1.1, the set of preferences needs to be both connected and transitive.

Also note in Figure 1.2 how indifference between two alternatives can be represented as a horizontal line. Thus, given the ordering of the alternatives in this figure, a legislator who preferred the reported bill to both an amended bill and no bill and was indifferent between the latter two would have a preference curve that fell from the first choice of the reported bill to the no bill position and then was horizontal to the amended bill position. Alternatively, given the order of alternatives in Figure 1.2, if a legislator were indifferent between

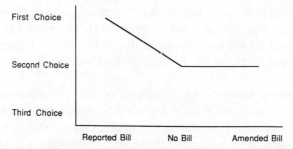

Figure 1.2.   Individual Preference Curve with Indifference between
Two Alternatives

the bill and an amended bill and preferred both to no bill, the curve would be horizontal between the location of the reported bill and amended bill alternatives and would then fall to the no bill alternative.

In both Figures 1.1 and 1.2, it can be seen that the preference curves have a single peak (in both cases, it is over the reported bill alternative). Note that the preference curve would also have one peak if the alternatives were rearranged with the reported bill alternative on the left, the amended bill alternative in the middle, and no bill on the right. More generally, a curve will have only one peak if, in moving from left to right, one never draws the line up after drawing it down. Although the number of peaks in a preference curve may seem like a strange thing with which to be concerned, Black (1958) recognized that the single peakedness of a set of preference curves is very significant; and because of this, one always tries, if possible, to draw curves that are single peaked (rearranging the alternatives on the horizontal axis if necessary to produce a single-peaked curve).

For one individual, it is always possible to find a way to arrange the alternatives, regardless of how many there are, so that the preference curve is single peaked. One way this can be done is to put the most preferred alternative on the left, the second most preferred outcome next to it, and so forth so that the least preferred alternative is on the right. It is also possible with some orderings of preferences to do this simultaneously for multiple individuals. For example, consider a hypothetical case in which the 435-member House is divided into three equal groups on a bill like the higher education bill. The 145 members of each of these groups might have the following preference orders:

Group 1:   reported bill > amended bill >   no bill
Group 2:   amended bill > reported bill >   no bill
Group 3:   no bill   > amended bill > reported bill

Given these preference orders, if the alternatives are arrayed on the abscissa so that *reported bill* is on the left, *amended bill* is in the middle, and *no bill* is on the right, it can be seen in Figure 1.3 that the preference curves for all three groups are simultaneously single peaked.[11]

Sometimes, however, for a given set of preference orders, it is not possible to represent all the orders simultaneously with single-peaked preference curves. Consider, for example, that if instead of the preference orders seen in Figure 1.3, the preference orders for the three groups are as follows:

Group 1: reported bill > amended bill > no bill

Group 2: amended bill > no bill > reported bill

Group 3: no bill > reported bill > amended bill

In this case, it is impossible to find an ordering of the alternatives which makes all curves simultaneously single peaked. Thus, in Figure 1.4, the preference curve for group 1 is not single peaked. With a different ordering of the alternatives on the abscissa, the preferences curve for group 1 can be made to have a single peak; but in the process of doing this, one of the other curves becomes non–single peaked. For example, in Figure 1.5, the order of alternatives is changed from that in Figure 1.4, and now group 2 has a non–single-peaked preference curve.

Single-Peaked Preference Curves and Equilibrium Outcomes

The basic reason for the concern in the spatial models of legislatures with single-peaked preference curves is that Black (1958) was

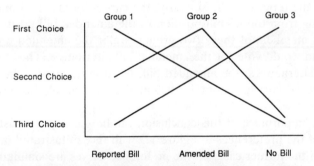

Figure 1.3. Preference Curves for Three Groups over Three Alternatives

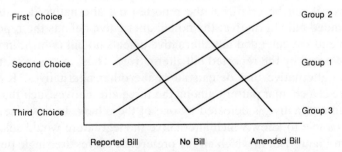

Figure 1.4. Preference Curves for Three Groups over Three Alternatives

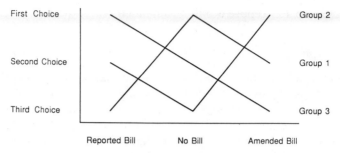

First Choice   Group 2

Second Choice   Group 1

Third Choice   Group 3

Reported Bill   No Bill   Amended Bill

Figure 1.5.   Preference Curves for Three Groups over Three Alternatives

able to show that if an ordering of the alternatives can be found so that all the preference curves are single peaked, the outcome under the median (or middle) peak will receive a majority against any other outcome.[12] Thus, in Figure 1.3, the amended bill outcome would receive the votes of groups 2 and 3 in a vote between this alternative and the reported bill alternative because the preference curves for these two groups rise in moving from the reported bill position to the amended bill position, which implies that both prefer the amended bill to the reported bill. Similarly, the curves for groups 1 and 2 rise in going from the no bill position to the amended bill position, and so the members of these two groups prefer the amended bill to no bill and would vote for the amended bill alternative. Thus, of these three alternatives, the amended bill, because it is under the middle preference curve, cannot be defeated by either of the other two alternatives.

The importance of this conclusion can be seen by contrasting the case of the preferences in Figure 1.3 with those illustrated in Figure 1.4. In the former case, all the preference curves are simultaneously single peaked, and a single outcome was shown to defeat each of the other alternatives. However, for the preferences illustrated in Figure 1.4, the curves are not all simultaneously single peaked. From these curves it can be seen that the reported bill alternative defeats the amended bill alternative; the no bill alternative defeats the reported bill; and the amended bill alternative defeats no bill (which, in turn, is defeated by the reported bill alternative). Thus, in this case, there is no alternative that defeats all of the other alternatives. Rather, there is a circular pattern among the three alternatives such that any given alternative is defeated by one of the others. In this case, it is impossible to know which alternative the legislature would select.

In Figure 1.3, in which all the preference curves are single peaked and the amended bill alternative is the one located under the median preference peak, this alternative can be referred to as an *equilibrium outcome*. Just as in economics wherein the intersection of supply and demand curves defines a market equilibrium, a voting equilibrium is one toward which the voting system will generally move if it is not there already; and once there, it will not depart.[13] Viewed in this way, the notion of an equilibrium is important for predicting what is likely to happen in a decision-making process such as voting. When an equilibrium exists, it is generally predicted that the process will move to the equilibrium position and then remain there. The equilibrium, in other words, represents the predicted outcome. It is for this reason that legislative decision models (like other models of dynamic processes) generally try to identify the conditions under which an equilibrium will exist and then to identify what the specific equilibrium will be.

In trying to determine the conditions under which legislative policy processes will or will not have an equilibrium, one must be careful to specify the kind of decision rule (e.g., majority rule) under which voting will be conducted. In the above example, it was assumed that all voting takes place as a choice between two alternatives. A variant of what is often called Condorcet voting, this is the typical type of voting specified in parliamentary procedure, and it will be referred to here as the *legislative voting process*.[14] With such a voting procedure, votes can be taken on whether or not to amend a bill, whether or not to pass a bill, whether or not to adopt a particular motion, and whether or not to end consideration of an issue. All these are dichotomous choices between only two options. This does not imply, however, that a legislature cannot consider more than two alternatives. Legislators can consider as many different alternatives (or motions) as they want; but with the legislative voting process, they must consider them two at a time.[15]

Thus, what Black (1958) proved is that if a committee or legislature is making a unidimensional decision under the legislative voting process, and if an ordering of the alternatives on the abscissa can be found so that the preference curves of all voters are single peaked, the outcome under the median (or middle) peak is a voting equilibrium that can defeat all other alternatives.[16] This equilibrium outcome is also the Condorcet winner or the Condorcet winning alternative. In Figure 1.3, the amended bill alternative is the alternative under the median peak; and hence by Black's theorem, it must be the voting equilibrium. It would be possible to rearrange the alternatives in

Figure 1.3 so that the amended bill alternative is no longer under the median peak; but in this case, the result would be that the preference curves are no longer all single peaked.

Note, too, that the examples in this chapter have used a discrete, and usually small, number of alternatives on the horizontal axis. The application of Black's theorem, however, is not restricted only to discrete cases because restriction on the number of alternatives considered is not a part of the assumptions behind the theorem. Because of this, the theorem is applicable to any number of alternatives, even an infinite number, as long as the preference curves over these alternatives are single peaked.

Because of the relationship between predictability and equilibrium outcomes, much of the rational actor theory of legislative decision making focuses on the conditions under which equilibrium outcomes will and will not exist. In this sense, the single-peaked condition is just one of many that can guarantee the existence of an equilibrium. However, as the analysis in Chapter 2 will show, a single-peaked assumption can be very powerful, allowing for the analysis of a variety of different legislative decision-making processes.

2

THE UNIDIMENSIONAL MODEL OF
LEGISLATIVE DECISION MAKING

■　■　■　■　■

How can a Black-type unidimensional model be used to analyze actual legislative decision making? As will be shown here, such a model is useful for examining both the outcomes of legislative decision making and the impact of various rules and structures on such outcomes.

Consider first how the model can be used to analyze legislative outcomes. Several years ago, the seven-member school board on which I serve was trying to determine the amount of a salary increase for superintendent of schools. Two of the members favored a $500 increase, one favored $1500, one favored $2000, two favored $2500, and one favored $3000. As there was no other issue involved, this was a unidimensional decision, and it seems appropriate to assume that all the board members had transitive and single-peaked preferences (e.g., the members who favored a $500 increase preferred it to an increase of $1500, $2000, or larger). Thus, it is possible to use the model of the previous chapter and represent the preferences of the seven members as in Figure 2.1.[1] By examining the preference curves, it can be seen that the median peak is the one over *$2000*, making that the predicted outcome of Black's median outcome model. In the actual case at hand, this turned out to be a very good prediction, because after much discussion and several votes, the board decided to give the superintendent a $2000 increase.

It might be thought that in a case like this, the members would simply split the difference between the high and low values; but the midpoint of the $500–$3000 range is $1750, and that was not the correct outcome. Alternatively, the members could have added all

21

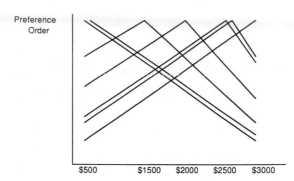

Preference
Order

$500 $1500 $2000 $2500 $3000

Figure 2.1.   Preference Curves of a Seven-Person School Board with Respect to
the Salary Increase of the Superintendent

their preferred positions together and divided by 7 to give the mean, or average outcome; but in this case, the yield would have been $1789, which again is not a correct prediction. Thus, in this case, there is fairly strong evidence that a Black-type median outcome model is the most appropriate and accurate way to characterize the outcome.

Note also that, in this case, it makes no difference in which order the alternatives are considered. Because all the preference curves are single peaked and the $2000 outcome is under the median peak, it can defeat any of the other outcomes in a majority vote. Thus, the $2000 outcome will win regardless of the order of voting, and this is generally true when all the preference curves are simultaneously single peaked.

As a second example of using the unidimensional model to predict legislative policy outcome, consider a hypothetical case of decision making in the U.S. House of Representatives. Assume that the president has proposed a new weapons system for the Army which will cost between $50 and $200 million dollars over three years (and assume that the actual costs are not currently known). It is known, however, that 178 members of the House are opposed to building the system whatever its cost, that 40 members favor only building a small prototype so that better cost and effectiveness estimates can be made, that 190 members favor the system if it can be built for $50 million or less, that only 17 members favor building it if it costs $100 million or less, and that 10 members favor it even if it costs $200 million. Note that these preferences are arranged in Figure 2.2 from *no system* through various partial systems to a full $200 million system. The question then is which position the House is likely to adopt if all the preference curves are single peaked. With 435 members, a House majority consists of 218 members. With a Black-type model,

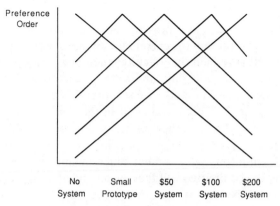

Figure 2.2.   Preference Curves of Five Groups of Legislators Concerning Five
Weapons Systems

then, one needs to find the position of the 218th preference curve
(counting from either side). Here, 178 plus 40 is exactly 218, so the
median peak is over the *small prototype* position, and that would be
the expected outcome.

Of course, it could be argued here that anyone can add 178 and
40 and get 218 and does not need a spatial model or Black's theorem
to do so. However, it is the logic of Black's theorem which allows
this addition to make sense. The assumptions from which the theorem
is derived allow one to predict that the 178 members who wanted no
system would vote in favor of the prototype alternative against all
other proposals except the one to build no system. Similarly, the
assumptions are that all those who wanted to build more than a
prototype would vote against the prototype in a vote against a more
than prototype system but would favor the prototype over no system.
Thus, the single-peak assumption provides a reason for adding 178
to 40 which otherwise would not exist. Note also that if all the curves
were not single peaked, the adding of 40 and 178 would likely produce
the wrong answer, as subsequent results will show.

Consider now a second use of a Black-type model which can be
found in the literature on legislative decision making. This concerns
attempts to determine what effects various institutional arrangements
have on legislative outcomes. Both Denzau and Mackay (1983) and
Krehbiel (1987), for example, used such a model to examine the
powers of committees to affect legislation. By assuming that bills can
be treated as unidimensional phenomena and that legislators have
single-peaked preferences, they can employ Black's theorem about
the outcome under the median peak to determine whether committees

will be influential in Congress. Consider, for example, Figure 2.3, in which the *horizontal line* represents positions on a single-issue dimension. Let Q represent the current law on the dimension (the status quo position) that remains in effect if no new law is passed. Similarly, let CM represent the outcome under the median peak for the committee on this dimension, and let FM represent the median for a full legislative chamber.[2] This means that in the committee, a majority prefer position CM to all other positions, and the committee would be expected to report a bill corresponding to position CM.[3] If there are no rules limiting full chamber amendments, the position CM reported by the committee will then be amended in the full chamber to position FM. Note, too, that in this case, the status quo position Q has no impact on the outcome, and this would be true regardless of the location of Q in the issue space. In this case, it is clear that neither the committee nor the status quo has any independent influence on the legislative outcome. The full chamber median FM would win whether or not a committee existed which reported CM to the full chamber, and FM would also win regardless of the location of the status quo position. Thus, this straightforward application of the median voter theorem shows that if committees are indeed powerful in Congress, it must be because of other characteristics of committees or the chambers themselves.

One set of such characteristics includes various sophisticated strategies employed by committees to win in the full chamber, and we will consider these in the next chapter. Another set includes the various rules and procedures governing the legislative process in the Congress. One of these, which is considered here, is a closed rule, which bars the full chamber from amending bills reported from committee.

In Figure 2.3, it was seen that with an open rule, the committee bill was amended in the full chamber to the position FM and that the status quo position Q had no impact on the result. However, if a closed rule were in effect for this case, both these conclusions would become invalid. With a closed rule, the full chamber cannot amend position CM, and so full chamber actors are faced with a choice between accepting or rejecting CM. Moreover, if CM is rejected, the

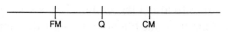

Figure 2.3.   Location of the Floor Median (*FM*), the Status Quo (*Q*), and the
Committee Median (*CM*) in a One-Dimensional Issue Space

status quo position Q wins by default. In Figure 2.3, it can be seen that the status quo Q is between *FM* and *CM*, which means that a full chamber majority prefer Q to *CM*; so in this case, they could be expected to reject the committee bill.

Consider now the case illustrated in Figure 2.4, in which Q is not between *CM* and *FM*. As in the previous case, Black's theorem predicts that the committee would report *CM* to the full chamber. In this case, however, it can be seen that *CM* is closer to *FM* than is Q, so a full chamber majority would prefer *CM* to Q and would vote to adopt *CM*. Thus, in this case, the committee wins, and this result was made possible by the closed rule barring the full chamber from amending *CM* to position *FM*. The presence or absence of such a rule, in other words, can determine outcomes as much as the preferences of the actors themselves. Moreover, note that the closed rule and others like it also make the position of the status quo an important factor in determining outcomes. With no restrictive rules, the position of the status quo was irrelevant; but with a restrictive rule, this position can be important. In particular, for the examples here, a status quo between *CM* and *FM* will always be adopted under a closed rule because a full chamber majority prefers such a Q to *CM*. Similarly, when *CM* is between *FM* and Q, as in Figure 2.4, Q will never be adopted because *CM* is closer to *FM* than is Q. Finally, when *FM* is between *CM* and Q, the outcome will be Q if the preference curves of full chamber actors fall more rapidly in the *FM–CM* interval than they do in the *FM–Q* interval, and it will be *CM* if they fall faster in *FM–Q* than in *FM–CM*.

The Problem of Non–Single-Peaked Preference Curves

In the preceding section, it was shown how a simple, unidimensional spatial model can be used to represent legislative decision making. In doing this, it was assumed that the alternatives could be arranged on the single dimension so that the preference curves of all the legislators were single peaked. In turn, this allowed the use of Black's theorem to predict which alternative would be chosen. What happens when the single-peaked assumption does not hold, and it is

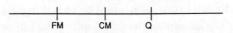

Figure 2.4. Location of the Floor Median (*FM*), the Status Quo (*Q*), and the Committee Median (*CM*) in a One-Dimensional Issue Space

not possible to find an arrangement of alternatives which produces single-peaked preference curves for all actors? In the higher education bill, for example, such would be the case if many but not all of the members who wanted to provide more money for student loans ranked positions lower, the less money they provided, but some also preferred a "do it right or don't do it at all" philosophy and ranked spending no money second to spending a great deal of money. There is no way the alternatives on this dimension can be arranged so that the preference curves of both sets of legislators are simultaneously single peaked.

Note first that single peakedness is a sufficient, but not a necessary, condition for a stable equilibrium outcome in unidimensional decision making. This means that if all the curves are single peaked, a stable outcome is predicted to exist, but such an outcome *might* also occur when all the curves are not single peaked. Because of this, nothing very drastic may happen if all the preference curves are not single peaked. However, since the additional conditions needed to guarantee an equilibrium (see Sen and Pattanaik 1969) are fairly stringent and are seldom likely to occur, it appears that majority voting schemes are likely to produce unpredictable results when preference curves are not single peaked.[4]

As a simple illustration of the problems that can result from majority voting processes when all the curves are not single peaked, consider again a simple three-person legislature weighing three different alternatives. Assume that the preferences of the three legislators for the three alternatives are as follows:

$$\text{Legislator 1:} \quad X > Y > Z$$
$$\text{Legislator 2:} \quad Y > Z > X$$
$$\text{Legislator 3:} \quad Z > X > Y$$

There is no arrangement of these three alternatives on the horizontal axis which will produce single-peaked preferences for all three legislators. As in Figure 1.4 of Chapter 1, one of the curves will always have more than one peak. Here, let alternative Z be the status quo position, and assume that this three-person legislature uses the legislative voting process whereby all votes are between only two alternatives. What outcome will be adopted?

In a legislature like Congress, the status quo motion is voted on last—that is, the final vote is on whether or not to pass the bill, which is equivalent to a decision between adopting the bill or the status quo of no bill. Thus, here, if legislator 1 first proposes that X be adopted, and legislator 2 then proposes Y (e.g., as an amendment to X), the first vote will be between X and Y. Legislators 1 and 3 prefer X to Y, so the outcome of this first vote will be X (i.e., the amendment is defeated). Now, X is put against the status quo Z, and because legislators 2 and 3 prefer Z to X, they will vote against X, and the status quo Z will be implicitly adopted. This all looks fine, but consider now what happens if the order in which the outcomes are voted on is altered. Assume that instead of the status quo entering last, the legislative rules specify that after a motion is made, it is immediately put against the status quo. The winner of this vote then defines the new (or same) status quo, and a new motion can be made to change this outcome. In the example, this rule implies that if legislator 1 first proposes X, the initial vote will be between X and Z. As legislators 2 and 3 prefer Z to X, Z will win; and then, after legislator 2 proposes Y, a second vote will be held between Y and Z. In this case, legislators 1 and 2 both prefer Y to Z, so the final outcome will be Y.

Working with the non–single-peaked preferences given above, majority voting produced two different outcomes. In one case, alternative Z won; and in another, alternative Y won. The preferences were the same, and the same majority voting system was used both times, but two different outcomes resulted when all that changed were the rules specifying the order in which votes would occur. Thus, in this case, it is impossible to predict which outcome will be adopted from the preferences of the three legislators; one also needs to know the order in which the alternatives will be considered. The basic reason for this outcome can be seen by examining closely the preference orders of the three legislators. A majority prefers X to Y, another majority prefers Y to Z, and still a third majority prefers Z to X. Here, the group level preference ordering is intransitive. Thus, an intransitive social ordering results from the voting system even though all the individuals held transitive individual preference orderings. As a whole, the legislature in this case cannot decide what outcome to enact. Whichever alternative is chosen, one majority will prefer something else: if X is chosen, a majority prefers Z; if Z is chosen, a majority prefers Y; and if Y is chosen, a majority prefers X.

Kenneth Arrow (1951) showed that in general, there is no way to guarantee a transitive social preference ordering for outcomes. A transitive order may exist with a Condorcet alternative that defeats all others, but one cannot be sure of this without violating some rules usually considered fundamental to democratic voting systems.[5] If the social preference orderings are intransitive, no equilibrium may exist, so that the outcome chosen is likely to be both unstable and unpredictable, depending upon such things as the order in which the alternatives are considered.[6] Because of the importance of this problem, almost all the subsequent work on legislative and other forms of collective decision making has in one way or another sought to deal with this *paradox of voting* or the *Arrow paradox*.

Another even more devastating demonstration of the paradox has been described by Plott (1976). He considers the case of three legislators and four alternatives. Let the preference orders for the three legislators be as follows for the four alternatives W, X, Y, and Z:

$$\text{Legislator 1:} \quad Y > X > W > Z$$
$$\text{Legislator 2:} \quad X > W > Z > Y$$
$$\text{Legislator 3:} \quad W > Z > Y > X$$

If the order of voting is such that W is first put against X, with the winner against Y, and then the winner of this second round against Z, the outcome can be seen to be Z (X defeats W, Y defeats X, and Z defeats Y). Notice, however, that all three legislators prefer W to Z. In other words, the outcome W that was unanimously preferred to Z lost to Z in the voting. Clearly, there is a major problem here. How, for example, would we explain why Z won when every legislator preferred W to Z? The answer is that Z won because it was one of the last two alternatives on which a vote was taken. Had Z entered first against either X or W, it would have been eliminated in the first round. Thus, given a set of preference orders, the order of voting on alternatives turns out to be the major factor in determining which alternative is chosen.

Note also that these problems are not just artificial, resulting from the preferences specifically used in the example above. These are real problems that can arise in real decision-making situations. Riker (1958), for example, discovered a case in which just such a problem arose. In 1953, the House of Representatives was considering the Agriculture Appropriations Act of 1953 where "the most significant and controversial subject was the amount of money for the Soil Conservation Service" (p. 357). As reported by the committee on appropriations, $250 million was allocated for the service. During full House consideration, Representative Javits (Republican, New York) offered an amendment to change this $250 million to $142.41 million. Representative O'Toole (Democrat, New York) then moved to amend the Javits amendment by setting the figure at $100 million. House rules prohibited further amendments to the O'Toole amendment, but did permit a substitute to the first (Javits) amendment and then an amendment to this substitute amendment. Thus, under the rules, Representative Anderson (Republican, Minnesota) was able to offer a substitute amendment setting the figure at $200 million. Finally, Representative Whitten (Democrat, Mississippi), the subcommittee chairman, offered an amendment to the Anderson substitute setting the figure at $225 million.

As is shown in Table 2.1, at this stage, there were five separate proposals before the House. By House rules, the first vote was held on whether or not the Javits amendment should be amended with the one offered by O'Toole. On this vote, the O'Toole amendment failed, so the Javits amendment was not amended. The second vote was then held on whether or not the Anderson substitute should be amended by the Whitten amendment. On this vote, the Whitten amendment failed. The third vote was thus between the unamended Javits amendment and the unamended Anderson substitute. On this vote, the Anderson substitute lost, and a final vote (before passage of the whole bill) was held between the Javits amendment and the original committee proposal. On this vote, the Javits amendment lost, so the original committee proposal was not changed.

By themselves, these various votes do not demonstrate the existence of an intransitive social preference ordering. However, as Riker (1958) noted (p. 358):

> From the fact that all amendments failed one might infer that a majority favored the original proposal. Nevertheless, one awkward fact casts doubt on this inference: although the largest amount stayed in the bill, the third largest amount (Anderson) beat the second largest amount (Whitten). From this fact one may reasonably suspect an intransitivity here, for if the largest amount were really favored over all others, and the amount was the dominant criterion, then logically the second largest sum should have defeated the third largest.

Further, from a more detailed analysis of voting patterns, Riker showed that none of the alternatives in this case could get a majority against each of the others. The committee proposal that eventually won, for example, would have been defeated by the Whitten amendment, but such a vote was never held because the Anderson substitute defeated the Whitten proposal, and it was not considered again. Similarly, each of the other alternatives could have been defeated by some other alternative, as Table 2.2 shows.

Thus, in this complex but realistic case, a paradox of voting existed in the House. Nevertheless, the House, by not putting each of the alternatives against each of the others could not discover the existence of the paradox, and the consequence was that no matter which proposal was adopted, a majority would have preferred another.

Table 2.1. Proposals before the House Concerning the Soil Conservation Service Appropriations in 1953

Proposal	Amount
Committee recommendation	$250 million
Javits amendment	$142 million
O'Toole amendment to Javits	$100 million
Anderson substitute to Javits	$200 million
Whitten amendment to Anderson	$225 million

Table 2.2. Winning Proposals before the House Concerning the Soil Conservation Service Appropriations in 1953

	Original	Javits	Anderson	Whitten	O'Toole
Original	X	R	R	C	R
Javits	C	X	C	C	R
Anderson	C	R	X	R	R
Whitten	R	R	C	X	R
O'Toole	C	C	C	C	X

As a second example, consider the case examined by Blydenburgh (1971) in which a sequence of votes allowed him to reconstruct the preferences of the members of the House of Representatives. In trying to balance the 1932 budget, the House was considering raising revenue by imposing a sales tax (ST), an excise tax (ET), or an income tax increase (IT). Ignoring those who were indifferent in preference to all three alternatives, Blydenburgh concluded that the following groups of representatives existed:

Group 1 (162 members): $IT > ET > ST$
Group 2 (38 members): $ET > ST > IT$
Group 3 (16 members): $ST > IT > ET$
Group 4 (69 members): $ST > ET > IT$
Group 5 (71 members): $ST > (ET\ IT)$

Here, the parentheses for group 5 indicated an inability to determine from their votes their preferences between the excise tax and income tax alternatives. A plausible interpretation is that all the members of this group were indifferent to the two alternatives; but if only four of these members were actually indifferent, a cyclical social preference order existed in this case whereby $ST > IT > ET > ST$.[7] In this case, the House adopted the excise tax alternative, the last alternative proposed, even though a majority preferred an income tax increase. Moreover, had the excise tax proposal been voted on first against the income tax alternative, it would not have been adopted.

Blydenburgh identified the existence of a cyclical social preference order in this case because there was a sequence of votes on the three tax alternatives. However, such a sequence of votes does not often exist, and therefore the cyclical majority problem will not likely be recognized by either participants or observers. In the hypothetical example above, the three legislators would probably not have recognized the paradox because they would not have voted first on X against W, then the winner against Y, the winner of this second round against Z, and Z against either X or W. Real-world legislative decision making would have stopped after selecting Z, just as the House stopped after adopting the excise tax.

The cyclical majority problem is usually illustrated by using relatively simple examples; but this does not mean that it is a problem only in these cases. In fact, it is known that the *à priori* probability of the paradox increases rather dramatically with increases in both the number of alternatives considered and the number of voters (Niemi and Weisberg 1968; DeMayer and Plott 1970; Gehrlein and Fishburn 1976). Niemi and Weisberg, for example, showed that for three alternatives, the *à priori* probability of a paradox with three actors is .056. This rises to .082 for fifteen actors and rises again to .088 for an infinite number of actors. In this case, it can be seen that the probabilities of a paradox rise but not very rapidly with increases in the number of actors. Now consider what happens if the number of actors is held constant at three, and the number of alternatives is increased. For three actors and three alternatives, the *à priori* probability is again .056. This rises to .111 for four alternatives, .16 for five alternatives, and .20 for six alternatives. For more alternatives, the probability continues to increase so that for many actors and many alternatives, the *à priori* probability of a paradox can be as high as .84. This means that for a realistic number of actors and alternatives in decision-making settings such as in Congress, the *à priori* probability of a paradox is well in excess of .50 so that it is much more likely that a paradox will exist than that it will not. Thus, the cyclical majorities problem is more likely to occur in complex real-world decision making than in the simple examples constructed to illustrate the problem.

Also note that if James Madison was correct in his analysis in *Federalist 10*, the probability of a paradox should be larger at the national level than at the state or local levels of government. Madison's basic argument was, "Extend the sphere and you take in a greater variety of parties and interests; you make it less probable that a majority of the whole will have a common motive to invade the rights of other citizens; or if such a common motive exists, it will be more difficult for all who feel it to discover their own strength and to act in union with each other." In more modern language, this means that the larger the geographic area represented in a legislature, the more likely it is that the preference orderings of legislators will differ from each other. In turn, this implies that it is more likely that not all of these differences can be represented simultaneously by single-peaked preference curves. On the other hand, the more homogeneous the area represented in a legislature (and to Madison, homogeneous was associated with a smaller geographic area), the more similarity is likely to exist, and hence the more likely the preferences can be simultaneously represented with single-peaked curves. It is thus more likely that a paradox of voting will occur in Congress than in a local municipal legislature (e.g., a city council or school board).

Finally, note that in these examples of intransitive social preferences, it has been shown implicitly that parliamentary rules can have an important impact on outcome. Thus, rules that specify the order in which the alternatives are voted upon or rules that limit the kind or number of amendments that can be offered seem to be as important as the preferences of the legislators in determining outcome. This is indeed the case; and as will be shown in subsequent chapters, a major part of the spatial theory of legislative decision making concerns the interaction of preferences and rules in determining legislative outcomes.

Conclusions

The unidimensional spatial model considered in this chapter is relatively simple, but it is sufficient to illustrate the general approach of spatial theory to legislative decision making. With the aid of a few simplifying assumptions, spatial theorists have sought to isolate the essential elements of the legislative decision-making process so they become susceptible to intensive logical and mathematical analysis. These efforts have been repaid by a deeper understanding of how legislative processes work and by an identification of a series of fundamental problems at the heart of any form of democratic collective decision making. In particular, there is a possibility that there may be no alternative that is majority preferred to all others. In such circumstances, legislatures may still make a decision, which implies that at times an outcome may be selected even though there are others that would defeat it in a majority vote.

In many ways, however, the unidimensional spatial model discussed in this chapter is not realistic in terms of real-world legislative decision making. For example, the model assumes that legislators always vote their true preferences. It also assumes that the issues involved in legislative decision making can be reduced to a single dimension. Although these are both serious problems, they are not fatal for the theory, for, as the next two chapters show, both can be adequately managed within its confines.

3

SINCERE AND SOPHISTICATED VOTING

■　■　■　■　■

The analysis in the previous two chapters assumed that legislators always voted their true preferences. It was assumed, in other words, that in a choice between any two alternatives, a legislator would always vote for the alternative that he or she preferred. This is variously referred to as *sincere voting* or myopic voting. Given that rational legislators are trying to attain the outcome they most prefer, this is how they would normally be expected to behave. However, in developing the rational actor theory and applying it to voting and legislative cases, it was discovered that there are times when such behavior may not contribute to attaining one's goals. There are times, in other words, when it may be rational for a legislator to vote against a preferred alternative. In contrast to sincere voting, such behavior is referred to as *sophisticated voting*.

To see when legislators have incentives to vote against motions they prefer, consider again the simple case of three legislators deciding among three alternatives in which the preferences of the legislators are as follows:

$$\text{Legislator 1:} \quad X > Y > Z$$
$$\text{Legislator 2:} \quad Y > Z > X$$
$$\text{Legislator 3:} \quad Z > X > Y$$

Assume here that the rules of the legislature specify that the first vote be between X and Y with the winning motion then put against Z. From the preference orders it can be seen that two legislators (1 and 2) prefer X to Y, so with sincere voting X would win the first vote. On the second vote, two legislators (2 and 3) prefer Z to X, so Z

would win the second vote and be the final outcome. Notice, however, that a majority (1 and 2) prefers Y to Z. On the first vote, 1 voted for X, but if 1 had voted for Y, Y would have won in the first round and then have gone on and defeated Z in the second round. By so voting, 1 is not voting his or her true preferences, but is better off because the final outcome of Y is better for 1 than is Z. Thus, in this case, 1 would have an incentive to adopt a strategy of voting differently from his or her true preferences, and this would change the final outcome from Z to Y. Neither of the other legislators in this particular case has such an incentive, but both would have if the order of voting had been different. For example, if the order of voting had been Y against Z and the winner against X, the sincere outcome would be X. In this case, legislator 2 has an incentive to adopt a sophisticated strategy and vote for Z on the first ballot instead of Y so that the final outcome is Z instead of X.

A useful way of examining when legislative actors may have an incentive to adopt sophisticated strategies was proposed by McKelvey and Niemi (1978). They showed that with a legislative voting process in which each vote is a dichotomous choice between two alternatives, the set of all possible decisions can be diagramed as a decision tree as in Figure 3.1. Each of the nodes in this tree represents a decision point, and the two branches emanating from each node represent the two alternatives from which a decision is to be made. Thus, with a voting order of X against Y and the winner against Z, the first decision (at the top of the tree) is between X and Y. If X wins, the second decision will be between X and Z, whereas if Y wins, the second decision will be between Y and Z.

To use this decision tree to analyze sophisticated voting, note first that on the last vote all actors will vote sincerely since at this point there is nothing to be gained by voting differently from one's preference. By examining the preference orders it can be seen that in the X–Z choice, Z will win, and in the Y–Z choice, Y will win. These

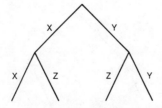

Figure 3.1.   Decision Tree for Three Alternatives under the Legislative
Voting Process

outcomes can then be used to replace the alternatives one step up on the tree. Thus, the previous tree now takes on the appearance given in Figure 3.2, with Z replacing X, for the final outcome in going down the left branch is really Z and not X. As Y wins on the right branch, it is not replaced. Now it can be seen that the first choice is really between Z and Y, not X and Y. By seeing this, legislator 1 knows that a vote for his or her true preference of X on the first vote will result in a victory for Z, his or her least preferred outcome; but by adopting a sophisticated strategy and voting for Y on the first vote, the outcome will then be Y instead of Z, which is better for legislator 1 than is outcome Z.

Note that in adopting a sophisticated strategy, 1 is better off, and 3 is considerably worse off. Thus, sophisticated strategies benefit those who use them (otherwise they would not use them) and can hurt those who do not, or do not have an opportunity, to use them (and here 3 did not have an opportunity; voting for Y instead of X on the first vote would not have altered the final outcome).

As a more complicated and realistic illustration of sophisticated voting, consider a bill B reported by a committee in the House of Representatives. Under the rules of the House (Rule 19):

> When a motion or proposition is under consideration a motion to amend and a motion to amend that amendment shall be in order, and it shall also be in order to offer a further amendment by way of a substitute, to which one amendment may be offered, but which shall not be voted on until the original matter is perfected. . . .

As in Riker's example in Chapter 2, this means that while considering bill B, an amendment A can be proposed as can an amendment A' to the original amendment A; but further, a substitute amendment S and an amendment to this substitute, S', can also be proposed. Finally, if none of these pass, the status quo position Q remains in effect. Thus, in this case, there are six possible outcomes: B, A, A', S, S', and Q.

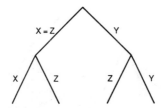

Figure 3.2.   Calculating Sophisticated Voting Strategies from a Decision Tree

Note also that the rule above, along with other House rules, specifies the order in which the House will vote on these various motions. The first vote will be on whether or not to amend the amendment A. Thus, the first vote will be between A and A'. A second vote will then be held between the substitute S and the amendment to the substitute, S'. The winner of this vote is then put against the winner of the first vote so that either S or S' will be put against either A or A'. The winner of this vote is then pitted against B, the original bill. Finally, this last winner is put against the status quo position Q. This whole voting order is shown in Figure 3.3.

Assume now that there are five actors (or sets of actors) with the following preference orders:

Legislator 1: $Q > A > A' > S \; > S' > B$

Legislator 2: $A \; > Q > A' > S \; > S' > B$

Legislator 3: $A' > S \; > A \; > S' \; > Q > B$

Legislator 4: $S' > B > S \; > A' > A > Q$

Legislator 5: $B \; > S' > S \; > A' > A > Q$

By arranging these motions on a horizontal axis in the order Q, A, A', S, S', B, it can be seen that the preferences of all five legislators can be represented by single-peaked preference curves and that the median peak is over the alternative A'. A', in other words, can get a majority against each of the other alternatives and is thus the Condorcet winner. Will A' be the outcome here? If all five legislators vote sincerely, the outcomes at each stage of the process are given in Table 3.1. In the table it can be seen that A' is the expected outcome with all legislators voting sincerely on each vote.

Consider now what happens if legislator 4 votes in a sophisticated fashion on the first vote, voting for A rather than A', while all the others vote sincerely. A' is now eliminated, and as Table 3.2 shows, the new outcome is S, which legislator 4 prefers to A'. Thus, by a sophisticated vote, legislator 4 has done better than he or she would have by voting sincerely. More importantly, however, what this example shows is that Black's median outcome prediction does not always hold when some actors vote sincerely and others engage in sophisticated voting.[1]

It can also be observed in this example that it was assumed that only one legislator engaged in sophisticated voting and on only one vote. However, what if they all engaged in such behavior? In the first vote, for example, legislator 2, anticipating legislator 4's sophisticated vote, might also cast a sophisticated vote and thereby change the

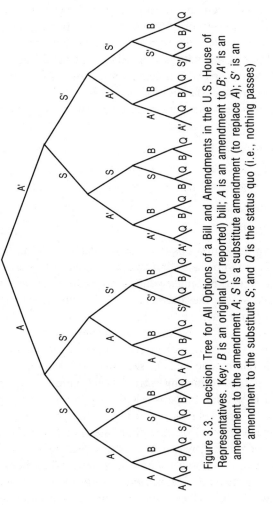

Figure 3.3.   Decision Tree for All Options of a Bill and Amendments in the U.S. House of Representatives. Key: *B* is an original (or reported) bill; *A* is an amendment to *B*; *A'* is an amendment to the amendment *A*; *S* is a substitute amendment (to replace *A*); *S'* is an amendment to the substitute *S*; and *Q* is the status quo (i.e., nothing passes)

Table 3.1. Outcome with Sincere Voting by All Legislators

Stage	Alternatives	Outcome	Winning Coalition
1	A, A'	A'	3, 4, 5
2	S, S'	S	1, 2, 3
3	S, A'	A'	1, 2, 5
4	B, A'	A'	1, 2, 3
5	Q, A'	A'	3, 4, 5

Table 3.2. Outcomes with One Sophisticated Vote

Stage	Alternatives	Outcome	Winning Coalition
1	A, A'	A	1, 2, 4
2	S, S'	S	1, 2, 3
3	S, A	S	3, 4, 5
4	S, B	S	1, 2, 3
5	Q, S	S	3, 4, 5

outcome at this stage back to A'. As noted previously, by starting at the bottom of the tree in Figure 3.3 and assuming that everyone votes his or her true preference on this last vote, one can calculate the winner for each pair. Thus, at the bottom and left side of the tree in Figure 3.3, the choice is between A and Q. As a majority sincerely prefers Q, this is one of the sophisticated equivalents for the decision point one node up on the tree. In the other one, immediately to the right, where B is against Q, the winner would also be Q. By replacing the option one step up with these winners and proceeding in this manner to the top of the tree, the winning motion when all actors use sophisticated voting can be determined.[2] In this case, the outcome is A', the same outcome that resulted when all used sincere voting. This outcome is not an accident, for with a unidimensional issue space and all preference curves single peaked, the outcome under sincere and sophisticated voting will always be the same. This phenomenon is easy to show by noting that at the bottom of the sophisticated decision tree, one of the outcomes will be the outcome under the median peak (here, A'). With all voters voting sincerely on the last vote, this outcome must defeat the one against which it is matched and will thus become one of the sophisticated alternatives on the next step up the decision tree. With sincere voting among the sophisticated equivalents at this next stage up, the A' alternative will also win and advance as one of the sophisticated equivalents to the next higher stage on the tree. By repeating this argument for each stage of the tree, it can be seen that the A' alternative will win at each stage, and hence the sophisticated and sincere outcomes must be identical.

However, when either the unidimensional or single-peaked assumption is not true, significantly different results can occur if legislators use sophisticated instead of sincere voting. In the case illustrated in Figure 3.1, for example, in which the preference curves are not all single peaked, the outcome when all use sincere voting is Z, whereas the outcome when all use what sophisticated strategies are available to them is Y.

For a simpler illustration of the potential use and importance of sophisticated behavior on legislative outcomes, consider the case illustrated in Figure 3.4. This is similar to the case in Figure 2.3 except that in this new example it is assumed that, as in Congress, all bills must be referred to committees when they are first introduced and that it is very difficult to remove (or discharge) a bill from a committee. Given the position of Q between the committee and floor medians, it can be seen that a committee majority in Figure 3.4 would be made worse off by reporting CM than it would be by not reporting any bill. This is because the floor would amend the bill to position FM, which is worse for a committee majority than is position Q (i.e., a majority of the single-peaked preference curves must fall between Q and FM for CM to be the outcome under the median peak). By not reporting any bill, a committee majority can virtually guarantee outcome Q, the status quo, rather than the FM position. To do this, however, the committee members cannot behave in a sincere manner and vote for their most preferred position; if they did, they would report a bill with position CM, which would get changed on the floor to FM. However, if committee members did not vote their true preferences, they could decide not to report any bill and thereby guarantee Q, which they prefer to FM. In the example in Figure 3.4, it can be seen that a committee majority would have an incentive to engage in such sophisticated voting and by doing so would force the floor to accept Q rather than FM. For this reason, the earlier conclusion that committees do not matter would have to be drastically altered. Only committees whose members use sincere voting strate-

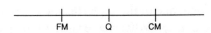

Figure 3.4. Location of Full Chamber Median (*FM*), the Status Quo (*Q*), and Committee Median (*CM*) in a One-Dimensional Issue Space

gies do not matter, whereas those committees whose members use sophisticated voting strategies can effectively block floor action.

This same situation can also be analyzed with the decision tree shown in Figure 3.5. With sincere voting, a committee majority prefers *CM* to *Q*, and so the first decision (in the committee) is *CM*. The floor then decides between the unamended bill *CM* and the amended version *FM*. As a floor majority prefers *FM* to *CM*, the decision on this second vote would be *FM*. Finally, on final passage, *FM* would defeat the status quo *Q*. Consider now the same case, but assume that the committee members adopt sophisticated strategies. By examining the tree in Figure 3.5, the committee members can see that at the bottom on the left, *Q* defeats *CM* on the floor, whereas on the next branch over, *FM* defeats *Q*. One decision up on the tree, the decision is thus between *Q* and *FM*, the sophisticated equivalents identified earlier. For this decision, a majority on the floor prefers *FM* to *Q*, so the sophisticated equivalent for the committee is *FM* on the left branch and *Q* on the right. A committee majority prefers *Q* to *FM*, and so *Q* would be expected to win in this case—that is, the committee does not report a bill. Thus, with sophisticated members, committees operating under the set of rules found in Congress can exercise gatekeeping power. To be enacted, legislation must pass through the gates of the committee, and by behaving in a sophisticated manner, committee majorities can force the status quo outcome upon a legislature that would *ceteris paribus* pass the *FM* position.

The gatekeeping power, however, is purely negative in one dimension: it only enables committees to prevent actions that a committee majority does not want undertaken. Without some other rule or procedure, committees cannot force the floor to pass anything other than *FM* or *Q*. Sometimes, however, other rules do exist. One

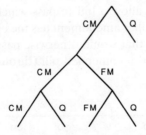

Figure 3.5.   Decision Tree for Committee Median (*CM*)–Full Chamber Median (*FM*) Decision Making

such rule in Congress is a closed rule for amendments. Under a closed rule, a bill reported from a committee cannot be amended on the floor—that is, the floor has a choice between the committee bill or no bill (i.e., the status quo). In the case illustrated in Figure 3.4 in which the status quo was between the floor median and committee median, the status quo would win because a floor majority preferred position Q to the position CM that the committee would report, and under a closed rule the floor cannot amend this position.[3] Consider, however, the case illustrated in Figure 3.6 in which the status quo is not between the committee and floor medians. Note here that a committee majority would have an incentive to report a bill under an open rule, because even if it is amended to position FM, that position is preferred to the status quo by a committee majority. Under an open rule in which there are no prohibitions about offering amendments, this is exactly what would happen. However, what if the committee could get a closed rule barring floor amendments? If the legislator whose preference peak is over FM prefers CM to Q, the committee could report CM, and it would then also pass on the floor. However, if this legislator prefers Q to CM, a sophisticated committee could find the point between CM and FM which this legislator just barely prefers to Q (e.g., the point SO) and report a bill at that position. With a closed rule, this bill would then pass on the floor.

Thus, in contrast to the negative gatekeeping power, closed rules provide sophisticated committees with the positive power to force the floor to pass bills that it otherwise would not.

Sophisticated Voting and Saving and Killer Amendments

Another way in which the concept of sophisticated voting can be used to examine legislative decision making is in the analysis of saving and killer amendments (Enelow 1981). A saving amendment is one that, if adopted, will allow a bill to pass which otherwise would be defeated, whereas a killer amendment has the opposite effect, leading to the defeat of a bill that would otherwise pass. Letting B represent an unamended bill, B' an amended bill (through the adoption of an

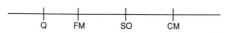

Figure 3.6. Location of the Status Quo (Q), the Full Chamber Median (FM), the Committee Median (CM), and the point SO, Barely Preferred by a Full Chamber Majority to Q

amendment A to bill B), and Q the status quo of no bill, the cases of saving and killer amendments can be represented using the decision tree in Figure 3.7. In this figure, the decision tree on the left represents the choice of legislators if no amendment is offered, whereas the tree on the right describes the choices available once an amendment has been offered.

For an amendment to be a saving one, it must be true in the left tree of Figure 3.7 that a majority prefers the status quo Q to the unamended bill B; in the right tree, a majority again must prefer Q to B and must also prefer amended bill B' to the status quo Q. This still leaves open the question of whether or not B' is preferred to B. As will be seen below, the answer to this question is important.

In contrast to a saving amendment, a killer amendment exists if, in the left decision tree, a majority prefers the bill to the status quo whereas in the right tree a majority again prefers B to Q but also prefers Q to B'. As above, this situation leaves open the important question of whether or not B' is preferred to B.

To examine saving and killer amendments, consider first the case in which all legislators vote sincerely. Consider, for example, the case of a three-person legislature in which the preference orders for B, B', and Q are as follows:

$$\text{Legislator 1:} \quad B' > Q > B$$
$$\text{Legislator 2:} \quad Q > B' > B$$
$$\text{Legislator 3:} \quad B > B' > Q$$

In this case, a majority of 1 and 2 prefers Q to B, and a majority of 1 and 3 also prefers B' to Q. Legislator 1 in this case would have an incentive to propose an amendment changing B to B'; with sincere voting such an amendment would pass because on the first vote, a majority prefers B' to B, and on the second, a majority prefers B' to Q. Thus, B' would pass and save the bill from defeat.

Should B' in this example be called a saving amendment? The concept of a saving amendment seems to imply that a majority would

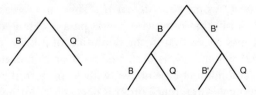

Figure 3.7. Decision Tree for Saving and Killer Amendments

have preferred B to B' rather than B' to B. In fact, if B' is preferred to B, B' is preferred to Q, and Q is preferred to B, the social preference order is $B' > Q > B$. In this case, B' is the Condorcet winning alternative that defeats all of the other motions. As it seems farfetched to call a Condorcet winning alternative a saving amendment, the previously given definition of a saving amendment is ambiguous and needs to be revised so that a saving amendment is one in which (1) a majority prefers Q to B; (2) a majority prefers B' to Q; and (3) a majority prefers B to B'.

Two important consequences follow from this revised definition. First, if B is preferred to B', Q is preferred to B, and B' is preferred to Q, then the social preference order must be $B > B' > Q > B$. This in an intransitive social preference ordering, and the implication of the revised definition is that saving amendments are only possible when an intransitive social ordering exists. In turn, this implies that the existence of a saving amendment in any empirical situation implies the existence of an intransitive social ordering among the legislators.

The second consequence of the revised and more precise definition of a saving amendment is that with sincere voting, a saving amendment can never be passed.[4] With the bill B preferred to the amended bill B' by a majority of sincere voters, B will defeat B' (and then be defeated by Q). A further implication then is that if a saving amendment does pass in a legislature, the legislators cannot have been voting sincerely.

Consider now the case of three legislators with the following preference orders:

Legislator 1: $Q > B' > B$
Legislator 2: $B > Q > B'$
Legislator 3: $B' > B > Q$

Here a majority prefers B to Q, Q to B' and B' to B. The fact that B is preferred to Q and Q is preferred to B' implies that the amendment changing B to B' is a killer amendment. Given the preference orders, legislator 1 has an incentive to offer an amendment changing B into B'; with sincere voting, the amendment would be passed, and the status quo Q would then defeat B'. Thus, in the case of a killer amendment, a bill that otherwise would pass is defeated.

Earlier it was noted that in the definition of a killer amendment, it was unclear whether B' is preferred to B or B is preferred to B'. In the killer amendment case above, with B' preferred by a majority to B, the aggregate preference order is necessarily intransitive. Thus,

Q is preferred to B', B' is preferred to B, but B is preferred to Q so that the social preference order of $B > Q > B' > B$ is intransitive. The alternative is that B is preferred by a majority to B'; in this case, however, with B preferred to Q and Q preferred to B', the social preference order is $B > Q > B'$, and B is the Condorcet winning alternative. As no option can defeat a Condorcet winner, the amendment creating B' from B cannot be a killer amendment. Thus, for a killer amendment to exist, it must be true that B' is preferred by a majority to B; and as was seen earlier for saving amendments, this implies that a killer amendment can only exist if the amendment creates an intransitive social ordering. However, here, with a majority preferring B' to B, a killer amendment can pass only if all vote sincerely.

Thus, it has been seen that both saving and killer amendments can only exist when they create an intransitive social ordering. Further, sincere voting legislators will always pass a killer amendment but will never pass a saving amendment. What happens, however, if legislators do not adopt sincere voting strategies and instead use sophisticated ones?

To answer this question, note first that the more precise definitions of saving and killer amendments are independent of the voting strategies used. Thus, it is still true that with the revised definitions, saving and killer amendments can only exist if they create intransitive social orderings.

To examine sophisticated voting in the case of a saving amendment, consider the case of three legislators whose preference orders are as follows:

Legislator 1: $B' > Q > B$
Legislator 2: $Q > B > B'$
Legislator 3: $B > B' > Q$

It can be seen here that a majority prefers Q to B and B' to Q, so B' meets the preliminary criteria for being a saving amendment. Also, since a majority prefers B to B', the additional criterion for a saving amendment is also met.

With sophisticated voting among the alternatives, the case can be analyzed using the decision tree in Figure 3.8. Starting at the bottom of the left side of this tree, it can be seen that a majority prefers Q to B (and on the last vote, all vote sincerely) so the sophisticated equivalent of the left branch is Q. Similarly, at the bottom on the right side, it can be seen that a majority prefers B' to Q so the

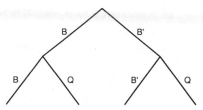

Figure 3.8.   Decision Tree for the Case of a Saving Amendment

sophisticated equivalent of this branch is B'. Finally, as a majority prefers B' to Q, the choice between the two sophisticated equivalents will be B'.

This example shows that in contrast to the case of sincere legislators who would never pass a saving amendment, sophisticated voters will always pass such amendments. An important consequence of this result is that if it can be determined that the revised definition of a saving amendment is satisfied, the passage of a saving amendment implies that at least some legislators use sophisticated voting strategies.

Consider now the case of sophisticated voting when a killer amendment has been proposed. To do this, consider again the case of three legislators with the following preference orders:

$$\text{Legislator 1:} \quad Q > B' > B$$
$$\text{Legislator 2:} \quad B > Q > B'$$
$$\text{Legislator 3:} \quad B > B' > Q$$

Examining these preferences it can be seen that B is preferred to Q, Q is preferred to B', and B' is preferred to B so that the definition of a killer amendment is satisfied. Again using Figure 3.8, it can be seen at the bottom of the left branch that B defeats Q, and at the bottom of the right branch, Q defeats B'. Thus, the sophisticated equivalents are B and Q, respectively. However, for these sophisticated equivalents, B is preferred to Q so that the killer amendment would not pass.

What is interesting about these results for sophisticated voters is the contrast they provide with those for sincere voters. Sophisticated voters will always pass saving amendments and never pass killer amendments, whereas sincere voters will never pass saving amendments and always pass killer amendments.

As an example of how the foregoing can be applied in real legislative settings, consider the case of a saving amendment examined by Enelow (1981).[5] The specific case he examined concerned the 1966 civil rights bill in the House of Representatives (H.R. 14765). As it was reported from the Judiciary Committee, the bill contained a provision that barred all "discrimination in the sale, rental, or financing of all housing." In assessing the situation on the floor of the House, it was seen by some supporters of the bill that it might be defeated because it contained a strong antidiscrimination-in-housing provision. As a consequence, Representative Charles Mathias (Republican, Maryland) offered an amendment that weakened the housing-discrimination provision. Instead of prohibiting all housing discrimination, the Mathias amendment ". . . permitted a real estate broker to follow the written instructions of a homeowner, even if discriminatory, in the sale or rental of a home, provided the broker did not solicit the instructions."[6] With the Mathias amendment, the decision tree for this case is given in Figure 3.9.

By examining both the votes of representatives as well as their statements on the floor before the vote, Enelow showed that a number of those who preferred the original bill to the amended version adopted a sophisticated strategy and voted for the amendment so that the status quo of discriminatory housing practices would not continue. With the support of these sophisticated legislators, the Mathias amendment was adopted, and in the final vote, the amended bill was passed. The Mathias amendment, in other words, was a saving amendment that did its job of saving the bill from defeat.

The second case examined by Enelow concerned the effective use of a killer amendment. This case was the 1956 school aid bill in the House. As reported by the Education and Labor Committee, the bill (H.R. 7535) "authorized $1.6 billion in federal grant aid for local school construction over a four year period" (Enelow 1981, 1080). Although federal aid to schools was a controversial issue at the time, it was initially thought that the bill as reported would pass in the House. However, Representative Adam C. Powell (Democrat, New York) offered an amendment to it restricting the funds authorized in

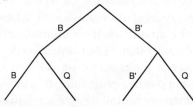

Figure 3.9. Decision Tree for the Case of a Killer Amendment (the Mathias Amendment)

the bill only to those states that complied with the 1954 Supreme Court desegregation ruling in *Brown* v. *Board of Education*. This amendment, if adopted, threatened to kill the whole bill because support would be lost from all or most of the representatives from states not in compliance with the *Brown* decision, who would not want to vote for a spending bill that would give their constituencies no benefits. This was exactly what did happen. The Powell amendment was adopted, and the amended bill was then defeated on the floor of the House. Consistent with the earlier analysis here, which states that killer amendments create an intransitive social ordering, Riker (1958) in his analysis of the Powell amendment suggests that it did, in fact, create an intransitive social preference order.

What is especially interesting about the Powell amendment case is that if legislators had adopted sophisticated strategies, the Powell amendment should not have passed. Earlier it was seen that killer amendments can never be successful when legislators adopt sophisticated strategies. Is this then evidence that such strategies are not used in real legislatures? Initially, this might appear to be the case, but from a more detailed analysis, Enelow concluded that many representatives were, in fact, using sophisticated strategies.

One reason that the Powell amendment passed despite the apparent widespread use of sophisticated strategies is that there was uncertainty before the first vote on the bill as to whether or not the amendment really was a killer amendment. As a consequence, some legislators who most preferred the bill with the amendment added and least preferred the status quo may have voted for the amendment hoping that it was not a killer amendment and that they could thereby gain their most preferred outcome. In doing this, these legislators adopted sincere strategies rather than sophisticated ones, and this fact may have allowed the Powell amendment to pass.[7] It is because of this uncertainty as to whether or not a particular amendment is a killer that Enelow proposed a probability (or expected utility) model for explaining the voting behavior of legislators who are faced with both killer and saving amendments. In such a model, different legislators will have different probabilities of adopting sophisticated strategies depending upon both their utility functions and their estimates of the probability that a given amendment is a killer or saving amendment. If such a probabilistic model is correct, then it also follows that there is a positive probability that killer amendments can pass and saving amendments fail despite a relatively widespread use of sophisticated strategies.

Conclusions

It has been seen here that there are times when rational actors may have incentives to adopt sophisticated strategies and vote against their true preferences. It has also been seen that there is some empirical evidence that real legislators sometimes do use such strategies. At the present time, however, it is unclear just how widespread the use of such strategies is in real legislatures. Nevertheless, the concept of sophisticated voting is theoretically important even if the use of such strategies is in fact limited. As a theoretical ideal concept, sophisticated voting is important, defining how purely rational legislators would behave and the outcomes that would result from such behaviors. These ideal criteria can then be used as yardsticks to assess the behavior of real legislators and the actual resulting outcomes.

4

MULTIDIMENSIONAL
DECISION-MAKING MODELS

■ ■ ■ ■ ■

The theoretical models examined in the previous two chapters assumed that legislative decision making could be represented in an issue space consisting of a single dimension. In some cases, this may be a reasonable assumption, but generally it is both theoretically restrictive and empirically false. It is theoretically restrictive in that a theory capable of dealing with only one issue dimension lacks an ability to explain what happens when legislatures consider bills that have multiple issue dimensions, and it is empirically false in that almost all the bills considered in real legislatures have multiple dimensions. In the case of the higher education bill discussed in the Introduction, for example, there were many separate issue dimensions combined into a single bill. There was a dimension for the overall amount of spending in the whole bill, another dimension for the amount students could borrow each year, one for whether or not students needed to pass a financial needs test, and many others. These are separate issue dimensions because the members of the House and Senate could change a provision in one of them without altering positions on the others. They could, for example, change the amount students could borrow each year without affecting whether or not students needed to pass a financial needs test.

As a consequence of both the theoretical and empirical limitations of unidimensional decision-making models, spatial theorists have developed more general and more realistic multidimensional models. The first step this development requires a means of spatially representing issue and preferences in a multidimensional issue space. How this is done is considered in the next section, followed by an analysis of how multidimensional spatial models can be used to analyze legislative decision making.

Modeling Preferences in Multiple Issue Dimensions

In the unidimensional models in the previous chapter, preferences were represented graphically by placing alternatives on one dimension and preference order positions on a second dimension. A straightforward extension of this scheme for the case of two dimensions would be to create a space of three dimensions with the alternatives on two of them and preference order positions on the third. More generally, such a representation implies representing n issue dimensions in $n + 1$ spatial dimensions. This is unnecessarily complicated, however, and it has not been adopted by spatial theorists. The preferred alternative for two dimensions (and one that can be mathematically generalized to any number of dimensions) is to use only the same number of graphical dimensions as there are preference dimensions and then to represent the preferences of a legislator as a function of distance from his or her most preferred alternative.

To illustrate, assume that the higher education bill consisted of only two dimensions: (1) the maximum yearly amount freshmen and sophomores could take out in guaranteed student loans; and (2) the amount that juniors and seniors could take out. It might be remembered from the Introduction (see Table I.1) that the Senate committee voted to set these amounts at $3000 for freshmen and sophomores and at $4000 for juniors and seniors. Presumably, the minimum that could have been approved was zero, and it will be assumed here that the maximum anyone wanted to approve was $7000. It is then possible to construct Figure 4.1 by letting the amount of guaranteed student loans for freshmen and sophomores define the horizontal axis and the amount for juniors and seniors define the vertical axis. Any combination of positions on these two issues can be represented by a point in the issue space. For example, the decision of the Senate committee can be represented by the point labeled *SC*, above $3000 on the horizontal axis and next to $4000 on the vertical axis corresponding to the position of setting the freshman and sophomore amounts at $3000 and the junior and senior amounts at $4000. This point, in other words, corresponds to positions on these two dimensions in the bill reported by the Senate committee.

Consider now a particular senator who was a member of the committee reporting the higher education bill. Assume also that of all the possible positions on the two guaranteed student loan issue di-

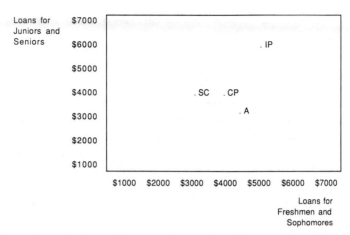

Figure 4.1. Preference Representation in a Two-Dimensional Issue Space

mensions, this senator would most prefer that the amounts be $5000 for freshmen and sophomores and $6000 for juniors and seniors. In other words, this senator would derive the most utility from a bill setting the limits at $5000 and $6000. This can be represented in Figure 4.1 by the position labeled *IP*. In the spatial theory of legislative decision making, this point, which gives the senator the maximum utility, is called that senator's *ideal point*.

The hypothetical senator would receive the maximum utility if a bill corresponding to *IP* were reported by the committee, and because *IP* is an ideal point, the senator would receive less utility if a bill corresponding to any other point in the space were reported. It also seems reasonable to assume that the senator would receive less utility from a bill setting the limits at $1000 and $2000 than at $3000 and $4000 because the former differs from the ideal point more than does the latter. In spatial terms, this is equivalent to saying that the senator prefers bills that are closer to the ideal point to those that are further away. Distance between points in the issue space is thus inversely related to the amount of utility the senator associates with various bills—the greater the distance from an ideal point, the less utility. This is why the various mathematical representations of utility functions over multidimensional issue space are frequently called *loss functions*: the greater the distance, the greater the loss in utility from what would be received if the ideal point were enacted.

Consider now the point in Figure 4.1 labeled *A*, which corresponds to the issue positions of $4500 for freshmen and sophomores and

$3216 for juniors and seniors. With a little high school geometry, it can be seen that the distance between *IP* and *A* is exactly the same as that between *IP* and *CP*.[1] Assuming that our hypothetical senator values both dimensions equally so that his or her utility changes as much with a given change on the freshmen-sophomore dimension as it does on the junior-senior dimension, the fact that *A* and *CP* are an equal distance from *C* implies that the senator would lose an equal amount of utility if either of these were passed from what he or she would if *IP* were passed. Letting $u(IP)$ represent the amount of utility the senator would receive if *IP* were passed, $u(A)$ the utility of *A* passing, and $u(CP)$ the utility of *CP*, this can be represented as $u(IP) - u(A) = u(IP) - u(CP)$. Equivalently, this can also be represented as $u(IP)$ − distance between *IP* and *A* = $u(IP)$ − distance between *IP* and *CP*.

The preceding formulation allows for a precise way of characterizing a senator's utility from any point in the issue space (or for any bill corresponding to these points). Moreover, it is possible to draw a curve in Figure 4.1 through all the points that are the same distance from *IP* as is *CP*. Given the assumption above about equal values (or weights) being given to each dimension, this curve will be a circle with *IP* at the center. This is because a circle is the set of all the points that are an equal distance from the center. In spatial models, such a circle is called an *indifference curve*. Because the points are an equal distance from an actor's ideal point, the actor would lose an equal amount of utility from the adoption of any one of them and would therefore be indifferent among them. Further, if two indifference curves were drawn at different distances from an actor's ideal point, the actor would prefer all points on the inner, or closer, circle to those on the more distant one because points on the inner circle would involve a smaller loss of utility. Thus, in Figure 4.2, a legislator would prefer all the points (i.e., bills) inside the indifference curve labeled *A* to those outside of *A* and would prefer those inside the curve labeled *B* to those inside *A* but not inside *B*.

In more technical terms, what is being assumed in the models in this chapter is that the multidimensional preferences of legislators satisfy the three general conditions discussed below.

1. *Continuity*. It is assumed that the utility functions of all legislators are continuous over the issue space. This assumption is made largely for mathematical convenience. It implies both that actors have preferences over all alternatives in the issue space and that a change in utility from one alternative to another close to it in the issue space

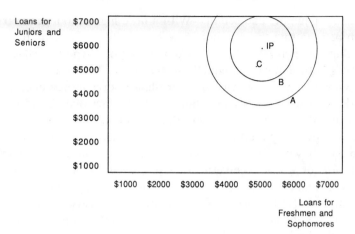

Figure 4.2.   Ideal Point (*IP*) and Indifference Curves in a Two-Dimensional
Issue Space

is small. Thus, in movements from an alternative to one nearby in
the issue space, preferences change in a gradual manner that can be
graphed by a smooth curve having no sharp changes.

2. *Strict Quasi-Concavity.* This is a compound assumption implying
both that the set of points preferred to or indifferent to another point
is a convex set and that indifference curves are very thin. A convex
set is one in which any linear combination of elements is also an
element of the set. For the purposes of preference models, this assumption implies that if a point *X* is closer to an actor's ideal point
than another point *Y*, then the actor prefers all points in the interval
between *X* and *Y* to *Y*.[2]

The assumption that indifference curves are thin sets is made in
part to simplify the mathematics but also to avoid the problem of
what an actor does when he or she is indifferent between two alternatives. With thin indifference curves, the likelihood of such an occurrence is small.

3. *Compact Preferences.* This assumption requires that the set of
points preferred by an actor to a given point be a closed and bounded
set. Said differently, this assumption implies that an indifference curve
can be drawn through any point, and this curve forms a boundary,
making the set of points inside this curve a closed set.

It can be seen that these assumptions about individual preferences
above are not very restrictive. Taken together, the assumptions imply
that preferences exist over all alternatives and that the utility asso-

ciated with various alternatives changes in a consistent regular manner over the whole issue space.

In terms of behavior, it is assumed at this stage that legislators vote sincerely so that when given a choice between the bills corresponding to two points, a legislator will vote for the point closest to his or her ideal point.[3] Thus, in Figure 4.2, it is assumed that the legislator, when faced with a choice between a bill/point inside the *B* indifference curve like *C*, and one outside *B* but inside *A*, would vote for *C*. Moreover, if an indifference curve were drawn through *C*, the legislator would prefer all bills/points inside this new indifference curve to *C* and would prefer *C* to any bill/point outside this indifference curve.

In the examples above, it was assumed that the senator valued the dimensions equally, but this is not a necessary assumption for spatial models of legislatures. Consider, for example, a case in which a senator's utility changed twice as much with a one-unit change on one dimension as it did on the other. Such preferences can be easily modeled by multiplying the distance on the more valued dimension by two. This has the effect of making the loss associated with a move away from the senator's ideal point on this dimension twice as great as a move on the other dimension. For example, if the senator with an ideal point of $5000 and $6000 in Figure 4.1 considered the freshman-sophomore dimension to be twice as important as the junior-senior dimension, he would associate the following utility with the point *CP*:

$$U(IP) - ((5000 - 3000)^2) * 2) + (6000 - 4000)^2$$

Adding in such weights, however, has the effect of changing indifference circles to indifferent ellipses, as is shown in Figure 4.3. In this figure, it can be seen that distance changes on the freshman-sophomore dimension are twice as significant as those on the junior-senior dimension. This is because a half-unit change on the freshman-sophomore dimension is equal to a full unit change on the junior-senior dimension.

The preference ellipses illustrated in Figure 4.3 are a special case because the major and minor axes of the ellipses are parallel to the axes of the issue space. In a more general case, this need not be true. In Figure 4.4, for example, it can be seen that the axes of the indifference ellipses are slanted with respect to the axes of the issue space. In this more general case, utility for any point (Y_1, Y_2) in the issue space can be represented by the following:

$$u(IP) - A(I_1 - Y_1)^2 + 2B(I_1 - Y_1)(I_2 - Y_2) + C(I_2 - Y_2)^2$$

where I_1 and I_2 define the legislator's ideal points; A and C are weights for each of the two issue dimensions; and B is a weight for the interaction between the dimensions (see below).

To understand this somewhat imposing formula, consider first the case in which A and C both equal one, and B equals zero. Multiplying anything by zero cancels it out so, in this case, the formula reduces to

$$u(IP) - (I_1 - Y_1)^2 + (I_2 - Y_2)^2$$

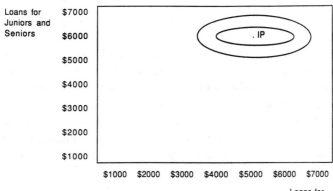

Figure 4.3. Ideal Point (*IP*) and Elliptical Indifference Curves in a Two-Dimensional Issue Space

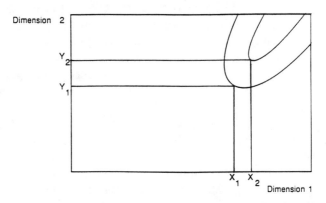

Figure 4.4. Elliptical Indifference Curves with the Axes Not Parallel to the Axes of the Issue Space

which is the formula for circular indifference curves. Similarly, in Figure 4.3, the case of elliptical indifference curves with axes parallel to the axes of the issue space can be represented by setting A equal to two, B equal to zero, and C equal to one. Thus, these other cases can be seen to be special cases of the general case represented by the formula above.

What is especially significant about the general utility formula is the $2B(I_1 - Y_1)(I_2 - Y_2)$ term. As has been seen, when B equals zero, this term drops out, and one is left with a simple additive model of utility whereby the total utility associated with some point in the issue space is the sum of utilities associated with each dimension. When this is true, preferences are said to be *separable* (Kramer 1972). Alternatively, when B is not equal to zero, the middle term does not cancel out, and overall utility is no longer a simple sum of utilities on each dimension. Rather, there is an interaction effect whereby the utility associated with a particular position on one dimension is affected by positions on a different dimension. An example of such nonseparable preferences would be a senator who would prefer to set the loan limit for freshmen and sophomores at $5000 if the limit for juniors and seniors were set at $6000 but would prefer to set the first limit at $4500 if the latter limit were only $5000. It can be seen in this example that the preference order on one dimension is affected by the expected outcome on the other. In contrast, a senator has separable preferences if he or she prefers to set the freshman-sophomore limit at $6000 regardless of the limit set on the junior-senior dimension. It will be seen subsequently that whether or not preferences are separable is important for what outcomes can be expected from legislative decision making.

As noted above, in Figure 4.4 the indifference curves are ellipses whose major and minor axes are not parallel to the axes of the issue space. Now consider the position labeled X_1 on dimension 1. For this position, the legislator most prefers the position labeled Y_2 on the second dimension (because his or her indifference curve is tangent to the line drawn through X_1 at position Y_1 on dimension 2). Now consider the position labeled X_2. Repeating the process, it can be seen that given X_2, the most preferred position on the second dimension is Y_2. In other words, the preference order of this legislator for positions on the second dimension is affected by positions on the first dimension (and *vice versa*). By repeating this analysis for the cases illustrated in Figure 4.2, it can be seen that this situation is not true in that case—the most preferred position on the second dimension is independent of, or separable from, positions on the first dimension.

Note that in all the cases above, consideration has been limited to just two dimensions. Two dimensions are convenient for illustrating the basic nature of multidimensional spatial models, and they are sufficient for demonstrating the nature of the problems that can arise in all multidimensional spatial models. However, there is no inherent restriction limiting such models to just two dimensions. By using the appropriate mathematical tools (most notably those of matrix algebra), any number of issue dimensions can be modeled, including the several hundred in the full Higher Education Act.

Note also that in the examples above, distance was calculated by squaring the difference between the points on each dimension, adding up these squares, and then taking the square root of this sum. This is the standard Euclidean distance taught in high school geometry. An alternative way of measuring distance is called the city block metric. (For a detailed analysis of city block metrics, see Rae and Taylor 1971.) As in an actual city in which the distance between two locations is calculated as so many blocks one way and so many more in another direction, a city block metric calculates distance by adding together the absolute values of the separate distances on each dimension. In Figure 4.5, for example, a senator with an ideal point at ($5000, $6000) would calculate his or her utility for the point ($3000, $4000) as follows:

$$u(IP) - |5000 - 3000| + |6000 - 4000|$$

It can be seen in Figure 4.5 that this alternative way of calculating distance (and thus utility) alters the shape of indifference curves. In the previous examples, in which a Euclidean metric was used, indifference curves were either circles or ellipses. With a city block metric, however, the indifference curves have the diamond shape seen in Figure 4.5.

An obvious question at this point is whether a Euclidean, city block, or some other metric is the most appropriate representation of the preferences of real legislators. In other words, why have two different metrics? Why not just use the "correct" one? For several reasons, there are no simple answers to these questions. First, as will be seen subsequently, the spatial theory never requires the cardinal measurement of all the preferences of legislative actors. In practice, the most one could hope for is to measure the preference order among only a few points in the issue space. It might be observed, for example, that a senator votes to amend ($3000, $4000) in the higher education

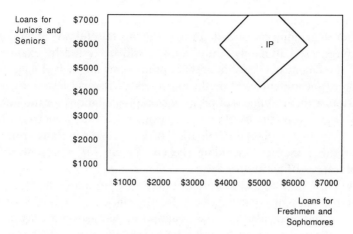

Figure 4.5.   Ideal Point (*IP*) and Indifference Curves for a City Block
Representation of Preference

bill with ($4000, $4000). Before voting, this senator might also make
a speech saying that although he or she supported the amendment,
even preferable to it would have been to set the values at ($5000,
$6000). From the speech, this senator's ideal point can be determined,
and from the vote, the preference order between two points in the
issue space can be determined. From these measurements, the preferences for any other position in the issue space can be determined
from the assumptions of the theory and, in particular, from the transitivity assumption. In this sense, any metric that is consistent with
the transitivity assumption, including both Euclidean and city block,
is theoretically acceptable. Empirically, it is not known and does not
need to be known whether one representation is better than another.
What matters is whether or not legislators behave *as if* their preferences were represented by some model, not whether the model is
right or correct in some way.

Second, note that rational actor theory is generally not concerned
with how particular legislators with a given set of preferences behave
in a given situation. The predictions of the theory can be tested in
these kinds of cases, but the theory itself is not about particular cases.
As any theory must be, the spatial theory of legislatures is about
general cases. Subsequently, for example, the impact of various rules
on the outcome of legislative decision making will be examined. This
analysis would not be of much value if it held for only a given set of
preferences. Rather, the theory should tell us what the impact of
rules will be for any set of connected and transitive preferences.

An implication of the foregoing is that theoretical requirements rather than empirical ones determine the most useful way of modeling preferences. Ultimately, these models will be tested by examining the agreement between theoretical predictions and actual legislative actions and outcomes. For the purposes of theory, however, what matters is the usefulness of preference representations for the further development of theory. For this reason, a Euclidean metric, which possesses many useful mathematical properties, is generally preferred over other metrics, including the city block, for representing the preferences of legislative actors.

Finally, note that the representation of preferences in the multidimensional issue space above is for the sincere preferences of legislators. As a consequence, an assumption that legislators act on the basis of these preferences and vote for the alternative that is closer to their ideal point is to assume that they use sincere, not sophisticated, voting strategies. Throughout the remainder of this chapter and in the next two as well, this assumption will be maintained. Sophisticated voting strategies in the multidimensional case will be considered in Chapter 7.

Modeling Legislative Decision Making in Multiple Dimensions

With the method presented above for representing preferences over alternatives on multiple dimensions, can a Black-type model be generalized to any number of dimensions? The most straightforward way of doing this is to generalize the single peakedness assumption so that legislators have single-peaked preferences in all dimensions. In Figure 4.1, for example, the preference curve for the senator with an ideal point at ($5000, $6000) has a single peak at *IP* and declines steadily the further one moves from *IP*.

For a small legislature of five members deciding a two-dimensional issue, the assumption of multidimensional single-peaked preferences produces a situation like that illustrated in Figure 4.6, in which the ideal (or most preferred) points of the legislators are labeled *A* through *E*. Assuming for the purposes of this illustration that all five legislators treat the two dimensions as equally salient so that their preferences are separable, the indifference curves of all five will be circular.

Note in Figure 4.6 that if the second dimension did not exist, this case could be modeled as a one-dimensional decision-making problem as in Figure 4.7.[4] In this latter figure, the positions of the ideal points of the five actors are noted, and it can be seen that they correspond

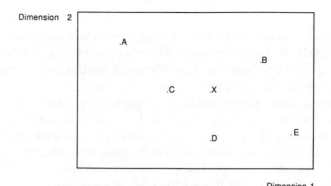

Figure 4.6. Location of the Ideal Points of Five Legislators (*A* through *E*) and a Central Point *X* (the Median in Each Dimension)

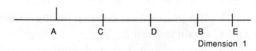

Figure 4.7. Reduction of the Preference Positions in Figure 4.6 to One Dimension

to the ordering, reading from left to right, of those in Figure 4.6. In this unidimensional case, the utility each legislator associates with different alternatives falls off steadily as one moves away from the legislator's ideal point, so all preference curves will be single peaked. As a consequence, Black's theorem predicts that the outcome under the median preference peak will be the majority winner, and in Figure 4.7, this is the outcome labeled *D*. Similarly, if the first dimension did not exist, the expected outcome would be that corresponding to position *C* on the second dimension in Figure 4.6. Does this mean that the alternative *X* corresponding to position *D* on dimension 1 and *C* on dimension 2 will be the outcome? The answer, it turns out, depends upon the rules of procedure which the legislature uses to make a decision.

Consider first the case in which the legislature uses what is called a *division of the question* rule. Such a rule specifies that the legislature consider only one dimension at a time. Because the preferences of all the legislators are separable, preference orders on the dimension not being considered will have no impact on the preference orders on the dimension under consideration. Thus, if the first decision is to be made on dimension 1 (ignoring dimension 2), the situation is exactly that illustrated in Figure 4.7. Moreover, on this single dimension, all the legislators have single-peaked preferences, and from Black's theorem it follows that the outcome under the median peak will defeat all other alternatives. Therefore, in this case, the outcome corresponding to position D, at which the median preference peak is located, is the expected outcome.

Having made a decision on dimension 1, the legislature now turns to dimension 2. Ignoring dimension 1, it can be seen in Figure 4.6 that the order of ideal points of the legislators on dimension 2 is A, B, C, E, D from top to bottom. Once again, this represents a set of legislators with single-peaked preferences making a decision on a single dimension, and Black's theorem again predicts the outcome corresponding to the median ideal point, which is C in this case.[5]

Thus, by considering the two issues separately, the legislature has arrived at the outcome corresponding to D on dimension 1 and C on dimension 2. In Figure 4.6, this implies that when combined, the legislature has adopted position X, corresponding to position D on dimension 1 and C on dimension 2.

Does this imply that position X is preferred to all other possible outcomes in the issue space? Unfortunately, it does not. If Figure 4.6 is repeated as Figure 4.8, and the indifference curves of each legislator are drawn through point X, it can be seen that majorities of legislators prefer all the points in the shaded areas to position X, and so any of these points would defeat X in a vote. Legislators always prefer positions inside one of their indifference curves to those on the boundary of the curve, and thus, the fact that the areas inside the indifference curves of a majority of legislators overlap implies that this majority prefers outcomes in the overlapping area to X.

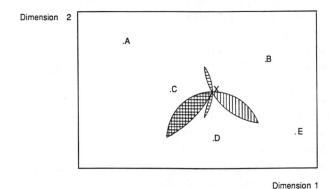

Figure 4.8.   Indifference Curves through X Defining Areas That Are Majority Preferred to X

Thus, legislators represented by positions A, C, and D all prefer the double-hatched area, which is closer to their ideal points than is X. For similar reasons, legislators represented by positions B, E, and D prefer the vertically striped area to X. In the language of spatial theory, the shaded areas in Figure 4.8 are often referred to as $W(X)$, the win set of X. Being inside a majority of indifference curves through X, the win set of X is thus the set of alternatives which would defeat X—or would win against X.

In the case in Figure 4.8, it can be seen that with a division of the question rule, it is impossible, once position X is achieved, to propose an alternative in (or element of) the win set of X. To get to the win set requires a change on both dimensions simultaneously, and this is not permitted under the division of the question rule. Under the rule, when making a decision on dimension 1, dimension 2 must be ignored; in this case, the position X corresponding to the location of the median ideal point D on dimension 1 is still preferred by a majority on that dimension. A similar argument holds for dimension 2, and it can also be seen that the position corresponding to the location of the median ideal point C on this dimension is preferred by a majority regardless of what point is selected on dimension 1.

One implication of these results is that if all the legislators have separable preferences, and the legislature is operating under a division of the question rule, a stable predictable outcome corresponding to the median on each dimension will result. This does not imply, however, that such an outcome could defeat all other possibilities in the issue space. Under the division of the question rule, it can defeat all other outcomes that can legitimately be proposed, but some outcomes—most notably those that involve a simultaneous change on both dimensions—cannot be proposed. More generally, what this illustrates is that procedural regulations like a division of the question rule can produce stable equilibrium outcomes. In the language of spatial theory, an equilibrium that results from the use of rules like division of the question is referred to as a *structurally induced equilibrium*.

What happens in the case in which no such rules exist? In other words, can an equilibrium exist without restrictive rules? To answer this question, consider again Figure 4.8, in which it was seen that all the motions in the shaded areas (the win set of X) can defeat X if they are proposed. Without a division of the question rule, such outcomes can be proposed; in the example, it can be seen that some legislators have incentives to propose them. Legislator A, for example, could offer a motion to adopt one of the points in the double-hatched area instead of X, and this motion would win with the support of legislators A, C, and D. Thus, in this case, X, corresponding to the median on each dimension, cannot be a stable equilibrium outcome; as a consequence, Black's theorem is not generalizable to multidimensional decision making in the absence of a division of the question or other agenda-limiting rule.

Consider now Figure 4.9, which is identical to the previous figure except that position X has been replaced by position Y, one of the points that was in the previous double-hatched area and was thus a point that defeated position X. Repeat now the analysis done earlier on position X by drawing in the five indifference curves through Y. Once again, it can be seen that there are several different shaded areas, the points in each being the win set of Y—points preferred by a majority to position Y. Thus, Y in Figure 4.9 defeats X in Figure 4.8, and there are additional points in Figure 4.9 which defeat Y. Some of these points, like Z, both defeat Y and are defeated by X so that the intransitive social preference order over these three alternatives is X defeats Z, Y defeats X, and Z defeats Y. This process could be repeated for every set of points in these figures, and one would come to the same conclusion: whatever point is selected, a majority prefers something else. The social preference order here is intransitive over all outcomes so that no equilibrium outcome exists.

From the point of view of the participants, this implies that there is not a single motion or bill (i.e., combinations of positions on the different dimensions in the legislation) which a majority prefers to every other motion. As a consequence, whatever bill is finally selected by a majority will actually be opposed by another majority favoring

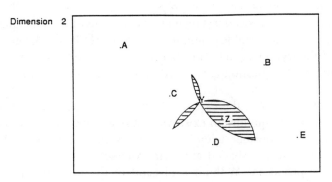

Figure 4.9.   Indifference Curves through Y Defining Areas That Are Majority Preferred to Y

another bill if a vote were taken between them. Moreover, from the point of view of legislative scholars and policy analysts, this problem implies that in cases of pure majority rule in which no restrictive rules exist, multidimensional legislative decisions cannot be predicted from a knowledge of the preferences of the actors. It can also be seen in Figure 4.10 that this result is not just an artifact of the legislators having circular indifference curves (or separable preferences). The indifference curves for the three legislators in this figure are drawn as ellipses with varying orientations in the issue space. For any given point in the issue space, such as the one labeled X, the elliptical indifference curves will overlap. In turn, this creates a set of points (the shaded area) which a majority of legislators prefers to X. If this process were repeated for one of the points in one of the shaded areas, a new set of points would be identified which a majority would prefer to this new point. Continuing in this way, it would be found that as with circular indifference curves, no point would be found that a majority would prefer to all other points, so that no equilibrium outcome exists. As a consequence, legislative outcomes will be unpredictable regardless of whether the legislators hold separable or nonseparable preferences. In fact, in both cases, every alternative in the whole issue space is an equally likely outcome.

This result is problematic because it implies that legislative decision making is both chaotic and unpredictable. As a consequence, a great deal of work has been devoted to determining the conditions under which a transitive social order, or at least a single most preferred outcome, will exist. One such condition was identified by Plott (1967). An equilibrium outcome exists if all the ideal points of the legislators

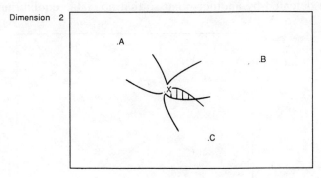

Figure 4.10.   Elliptical Indifference Curves through X and Area That Is Majority Preferred to X

line up just right so that one legislator's ideal point is at a place at which the indifference curves from pairs of other legislators are tangent to each other. This is illustrated in Figure 4.11 for a two-dimensional issue and a five-person legislature. In this figure, legislator *E*'s ideal point is at the exact place at which indifference curves for *A* and *D* are tangent and also at which the curves for *C* and *D* are tangent. In this case, position *E* can defeat all other points by a majority and is hence a stable equilibrium position. This stable equilibrium exists because legislator *E* obviously prefers position *E*, and only a minority of two prefers any other points in the space (because these points are only inside two, not three, indifference curves through *E*). Also note that even a small movement of any of the ideal points destroys this property of position *E*. The Plott condition for the existence of a stable equilibrium, in other words, is very precise, and the conditions must be met exactly, or no equilibrium will exist. Moreover, satisfying the Plott conditions appears more unlikely the greater the number of dimensions and the greater the size of the legislature. In turn, this makes it very unlikely that the distribution of points in any real legislature will ever exactly correspond to the Plott conditions.[6]

What is especially important about the Plott condition is that in the absence of restrictive rules like the division of the question, it is the only condition that will guarantee a stable equilibrium. This was shown in the now famous "Chaos Theorems" of McKelvey (1976, 1979) and Schofield (1978). They demonstrated that with the exception of cases that satisfy the Plott conditions, simple majority rule in legislative decision making will be globally intransitive. One thing this means is that except under the Plott conditions, any point selected can be defeated by another point so that no stable equilibrium will

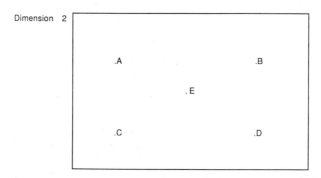

Figure 4.11. Plott Conditions for a Stable Equilibrium

exist. It also means that if there is to be an end to voting so that alternatives will not be continually put against each other, there is an initial motion that can guarantee that the final outcome at the end of voting will be a particular point. In turn, this implies that any legislator who can control the agenda and manipulate the order of alternatives can dictate the final outcome. Finally, the Chaos Theorems suggest that predicting what decision a legislature will make is extremely difficult, if not impossible, and certainly such predictions cannot be made solely by knowledge of the preferences of legislators. As the name of the theorems implies, legislative decision making may be nothing more than pure chaos.

Theoretical Chaos, Empirical Stability

The Chaos Theorems of McKelvey and Schofield are significant in showing that there is a fundamental problem at the heart of the legislative decision-making process: there is no equilibrium outcome toward which the final decision moves. Instead, the outcomes of legislative decision making may move anywhere in the issue space and be totally unpredictable. An alternative characterization is that legislative outcomes are unjustifiable in the sense that one cannot explain why a given outcome was adopted in terms of the majority rule concept at the core of democratic theory. In any given instance, an outcome was supported by a majority; however, except for the special case identified by Plott, there exist many alternatives that a majority prefers to the one selected. Thus, there is no reason for supposing that any given outcome is an optimal one or that it satisfies the normative criteria of democratic theory.

What is also interesting about the theoretical results above is the fact that they do not appear consistent with either the empirical or experimental evidence. Empirically, observers of real legislatures have not reported a great amount of instability or intransitive social preference orders in legislatures like Congress. In fact, what empirical studies like those of Fenno (1966), Manley (1970), Birnbaum and Murray (1987), and many others have generally concluded is that legislative processes are stable and considerably more predictable than spatial theory allows. Some scholars, in fact, have even developed theories—for example, the theory of incrementalism (e.g., Lindblom 1965)—which imply that stability and predictability are the norm rather than the exception in real-world legislative decision making.

A possible explanation for this discrepancy between theory and observation has been advanced by Riker (1958). He suggested that instability and intransitive social preference orders are not often observed because the voting rules of Congress (and many other legislatures) limit the number of votes taken and hence do not allow intransitive social preference orders to be observed. In the case of three alternatives, for example, congressional rules allow for only two votes instead of the three needed to establish the existence of intransitive social preferences. Thus, in the case of a bill B, an amended version of the bill B', and the status quo Q, Congress would first vote on whether to adopt amendment A and change bill B into B'. If the amendment is not adopted, a final vote is held between B and Q, whereas if the amendment is approved, the final vote is between B' and Q. In either of these cases, if Q wins on the last vote, a social preference of either $B > B'$ and $Q > B$ or $B' > B$ and $Q > B'$ has been established. Because in the first case no vote was held between B' and Q, it is not known whether the final social preference order is the transitive $Q > B > B'$ or the intransitive $Q > B > B' > Q$. Similarly, in the second case, it is not known whether the social preference order is $Q > B' > B$ or $Q > B' > B > Q$. From this it follows that there may exist more instability and intransitivity in legislative decision making than can be empirically observed.

Moreover, despite the limitations of congressional voting rules preventing the identification of intransitive social preferences, several actual cases have been found. In Chapter 2, for example, it was seen that Blydenburgh (1971) demonstrated the existence of a cyclical social preference order on the 1932 budget bill. For the three alternatives of imposing a sales tax (ST), an excise tax (ET), or increasing the income tax (IT), he showed that a majority preferred ST to IT and IT to ET. However, a majority also preferred ET to ST so that the social preference order was $ST > IT > ET > ST$. In this case, the House adopted the excise tax alternative, the alternative voted on last, even though a majority preferred the income tax alternative to it.

Similarly, as was also shown in Chapter 2, Riker (1958) identified the existence of an intransitive social ordering on the Soil Conservative Service appropriations bill in 1953. In this case, five different alternatives were considered by the House, and none was preferred by a majority.

Riker (1965) also analyzed the Powell amendment case, which was discussed in Chapter 3 as an example of a killer amendment. Riker, however, was interested in whether or not the preferences of the legislators implied an intransitive social preference order. In Chapter 3 it was also shown that with a revised definition, a killer amendment exists only when the social preference order is intransitive. Thus, if the Powell amendment had been a killer amendment, theoretically there should have existed an intransitive social ordering. From the fact that the Powell amendment passed, Riker inferred that $B' > B$. Similarly, from the fact the B' was then defeated, he inferred that $Q > B'$. Finally, to establish the social preference order between B and Q (which was not voted on), Riker inferred that it was likely that all those who voted for B' also preferred B. Also, by looking at the vote the following year, at which time the issue came up again without the Powell amendment, and passed, Riker inferred that a majority preferred B to Q. From these binary comparisons, Riker concluded that the social preference order was $B > Q > B' > B$, which is intransitive and cyclical.

Another occurrence of an intransitive social ordering, also discovered by Riker (1965), concerned the 1911 attempt in the Senate to pass a constitutional amendment providing for the direct popular election of senators. Similar attempts had taken place in the Senate as early as 1902 but had been unsuccessful because the Senate committee, in reporting the amendment to the floor, had included the following language:

> The qualifications of citizens entitled to vote for United States Senators and Representatives in Congress shall be uniform in all States, and Congress shall have the power to enforce this article by appropriate legislation and to provide for the registration of citizens entitled to vote, the conduct of such elections, and the certification of the result. (Riker 1965, 57)

Offered by Senator De Pew of New York, this amendment threatened southern support for the constitutional amendment because it gave the federal government the power to intervene in southern elections and to outlaw voting rules that discriminated against blacks such as the whites-only primary elections. So effective was the De Pew amendment in killing the constitutional amendment that the issue was not considered again until 1911. In that year, however, the Senate reconsidered the issue without the De Pew amendment and with the specification that "The times, places, and manner of holding elections for Senators shall be prescribed by the legislatures thereof" (ibid., 58). As Riker noted:

> This sentence was intended to guarantee the support of the South which remembered and feared the De Pew amendment and which by 1911

was thoroughly in favor of direct election inasmuch as all Southern Senators had been elected by popular vote for over a decade. Faced with this circumstance, the die-hard opponents of popular election proposed what was in effect the revival of the De Pew amendment, namely a motion to delete the foregoing sentence, which motion was known as the Sutherland amendment.

Thus, as the Senate began consideration of the issue on the floor, there were three alternatives: (1) the original amendment as reported from the Judiciary Committee (B); (2) the amendment as modified by the Sutherland amendment (B'); and (3) the status quo (Q) of no change in how senators were elected. In the vote on the Sutherland amendment, the amendment passed by a 50 to 36 margin so that the social preference order between these two was $B' > B$. In the next vote of B' against Q, the amended bill failed by three votes to get the required two-thirds needed for passage of a constitutional amendment. Thus, for these two alternatives, $Q > B'$. Riker then noted:

> To estimate the relationship of [B] (the original resolution unamended) to [Q] (no action) we can assume that all those who voted for the resolution on final passage also favored the unamended resolution. This is 54 Senators. In addition, ten Southern Democrats who has insisted on that protective clause in the original resolution which was removed by the Sutherland amendment, presumably favored the original resolution against no action. Indeed the protective clause was put in to assure their adherence to the original resolution. So the putative vote on [B] against [Q] is 64 to 24, which is more than enough to pass [B]. So the social ordering is [B] > [Q]. (ibid., 58–59)

Thus with $B' > B$, $Q > B'$, and $B > Q$, there is clearly an intransitive social ordering.

It can be concluded from these case studies that instances in which there is no equilibrium outcome because the social preference order is intransitive do exist in real legislatures. It is unclear, however, just how often they occur. It is possible that such cases are the exception rather than the rule. This would be consistent with the empirical observations of students of real legislatures such as Congress. However, it is also possible that the empirical observers have overlooked many nonequilibrium cases because the way issues are voted on restricts observers' ability to determine whether or not an equilibrium exists. Moreover, in procedurally complex legislatures such as Congress, there are many reasons why intransitive social preference orders may not produce unpredictable and unstable outcomes. As shown in the next three chapters, these reasons include agenda control by some actors, procedural rules that limit the chaos of outcomes, and the use of sophisticated voting strategies by legislators.

Some Experimental Results

Before considering these alternative explanations for the apparent stability of real legislative outcomes, it is instructive to consider the results that have been obtained in laboratory experiments of legislative decision making.

For testing spatial theories, experiments have two major advantages over tests in real legislatures. First, they allow for a great deal of control over the setting in which legislative-like decision making takes place. This allows the exclusion of many extraneous factors that make testing in real settings so complicated and gives experimenters great flexibility in manipulating variables and observing their effects.

Second, by allowing experimenters to induce preferences in their subjects, tests of the core preference-behavior relationship of the spatial variant of rational actor theory are possible. When known preferences exist in a very controlled setting, it is a relatively simple matter to observe how individuals behave and see if the behavior is consistent with the predictions of the theory.

In general, the experiments that have been carried out to test the theory have a common design. Most of them use a small number of subjects, generally three to nine, who are told that they will be participating in a group decision-making experiment. Consistent with the spatial theory, the group is to use various forms of defined parliamentary procedure (i.e., making motions and voting) to select a point in an abstract issue space. The issue space is abstract in the sense that the dimensions of the space are either not given labels or are given ones like X and Y. This procedure controls for any biases subjects might have were real-world issue dimensions used. To motivate subjects to care about positions in the abstract space, each subject is assigned an ideal point and is told how many points or how much money he or she will receive if the group selects this point as its decision. Selection of some other point in the space will then result in a lower reward according to a formula provided to the subjects by the experimenter.

Within this general framework, considerable variation is possible, but the key point is that by assigning an ideal (or highest payoff) point and a way of determining rewards for other points, a preference structure for each subject over the abstract issue space is created.

The experimenter can then observe the process by which the group decision is made and determine not only if the aggregate result reflected in the group decision is consistent with various theoretical predictions but also if individuals behave in a way consistent with their preferences.

To date, a number of different experimental studies have been undertaken.[7] Perhaps the most comprehensive and detailed among these are those conducted by Fiorina and Plott (1978). Their experiments involved having a group of subjects, using the parliamentary procedures of making motions and voting, select a point in an abstract two-dimensional issue space. In all cases, there were five subjects with assigned ideal points. By varying the placement of these ideal points as well as the way subjects were instructed to evaluate other points in the space, Fiorina and Plott established three different experimental settings that allowed them to distinguish among the different predictions of variants of the spatial theory. By also varying the amount of monetary reward in different settings, they were able to test for differences in how subjects behaved in low- and high-payoff settings. Finally, by varying the amount of communication allowed among the subjects, they were able to test for the effects of interactions on outcomes.

One important result was the difference in outcomes between the high- and low-payoff conditions. The existence of these differences suggests that subjects behave differently when there is more at stake. In particular, it appeared that in the high-payoff conditions, subjects behaved as predicted by various "egoistic" rational actor models. In low-payoff experiments, on the other hand, there was a much greater discrepancy of points throughout the issue space, and to the extent that there was any clustering, it appeared that subjects were much more likely to adopt a "nonegoistic" (or utility-maximizing) model and select the "obvious point" suggested by Schelling (1960).[8] To Fiorina and Plott, these results suggested "rather strongly that when individuals have a good deal at stake, one had better model their behavior via a theory which includes point A [the prediction of the egoistic rational actor theories] among its predictions" (1978, 584). In addition, they found that

> Overall . . . the differences in payoffs appear to be a more significant influence on the outcome of the committee process than differences in communication. Given high payoffs, the egoistic theories work well with or without communication. Given low payoffs, all the models work rather poorly with or without communication. (ibid., 585–86)

For this reason, the focus here will be on their high-payoff experiments.

As noted previously, Fiorina and Plott established three different experimental cases for their high-payoff condition, which allowed them to test predictions from different variants of the rational actor model. In their Series 1, subjects had circular indifference curves (implying separability of the dimensions), and a stable equilibrium existed. In their Series 3, subjects again had circular indifference curves, but no stable equilibrium existed. In their Series 2, the subjects had elliptical (nonseparable) preferences, and a stable equilibrium existed.

In both their Series 1 and 2, in which the distribution of ideal points implied the existence of an equilibrium, the experimental outcomes tended to cluster near the predicted equilibrium position. Thus, in their Series 1 experiments, the mean outcomes were (37, 68) with a standard deviation of 5.2 when communication was allowed and (38, 69) with a standard deviation of 8.3 when no communication was allowed. Both these means are quite close to the predicted majority rule equilibrium of (39, 68). Similarly, in their Series 2 experiments, the mean outcome was (60, 72) with a standard deviation of 7.3, which is very close to the predicted equilibrium position of (61, 69). These results in both Series 1 and 2 thus suggest that an equilibrium position, when it exists, exerts a strong influence on the collective outcome. The results further suggest that decision makers act as predicted by the theory. Notice too that the fact that the dimensions in Series 1 were separable and those in Series 2 were not apparently had no impact on the influence of the equilibrium. In both cases, the outcomes obtained clustered near the equilibrium.

Even more interesting are the results obtained in their Series 3, in which no predicted equilibrium existed. In theory, the outcomes in this case should be scattered widely over the issue space; but this did not happen. The mean outcome was (45, 62) with a standard deviation of 10.3. Although this standard deviation is twice as large as that for Series 1, indicating a greater dispersion of outcomes, these outcomes still clustered near the center of the ideal points. As Fiorina and Plott noted:

> In Series 1, the existence of an equilibrium is associated with a tightly clustered set of outcomes centered on the equilibrium. But in Series 3 the *nonexistence* of an equilibrium is *not* associated with experimental chaos. We did not notice any behavioral differences in the conduct of the two series; in particular, subjects in Series 3 appeared to have no

greater difficulty in reaching a decision than did those in Series 1. (ibid., 590)

This is a puzzling result. It appears from their reported observations that subjects in their Series 3 experiments behaved as predicted by the spatial theory. However, it is unclear why the absence of a theoretical equilibrium did not lead to a much greater distribution of outcomes in the issue space. It almost appears as if the subjects were imposing their own equilibrium close to the point at which it would theoretically be if one of the subjects had the ideal point assigned in Series 1. Inasmuch as they included no rules or structures to help induce an equilibrium, these results suggest that theories predicting unstable (or unpredictable) outcomes may be problematic, although the reasons for this are unclear.

A similar conclusion can be drawn from the experimental results reported by Wilson (1986). He was interested in whether or not differences in legislative rules affected outcomes. In particular, he designed an experiment to test whether the use of forward or backward moving agenda processes affected the final outcomes selected. With a forward moving agenda process, the status quo motion enters first so that it becomes one of the motions in the first vote held. In contrast, with a backward moving agenda process, the status quo motion enters last. Theoretically, with a forward moving agenda process, any outcome in the whole issue space is possible, whereas a backward moving agenda process constrains the possible outcomes to those that are majority preferred to the status quo. In Figure 4.8, for example, if X had been the status quo, the only possible outcomes would be those inside one of the four shaded areas that represent alternatives inside a majority of indifference curves through X.

Consistent with theoretical expectations, when a backward moving agenda process was used, all of Wilson's cases are either the status quo position or one of the alternatives that was majority preferred to the status quo.[9] With a forward moving agenda process, however, the outcomes selected were somewhat more scattered through the issue space. Consistent with Fiorina and Plott's results, Wilson concluded that "One point is clear; the outcomes selected here are not scattered throughout the alternative space" (404). Rather, he found that the "initial status quo [exerted] a powerful effect on the agenda" (405).

It thus appears that in the absence of restrictive rules, outcomes of legislative decision making do not scatter randomly throughout the issue space. Why this occurs, however, is not clear. More significantly, what Wilson's results show is the powerful effects procedural rules can have on legislative outcomes. As he notes, "very different patterns of outcomes arise from different procedural rules" (407). This is significant because, as shown in the next several chapters, a major focus of spatial theorists in the last decade has been on examining the systematic effects of various procedural rules on outcomes.

Conclusions

The analysis in this chapter has identified several major problems encountered when spatial models of legislative decision making are generalized from one to multiple issue dimensions. At the theoretical level, such a generalization leads to the conclusion that legislative decision making is chaotic in the sense that it is likely that no equilibrium exists; as a consequence, outcomes anywhere in the issue space are equally probable. However, both empirically and experimentally, with relatively few exceptions, such chaos has not been observed. Some of this lack might be due to the voting rules used in real legislatures which limit the ability of observers to identify the absence of an equilibrium. As a result, it is currently unclear the degree to which real legislative decision making is characterized by unstable chaotic outcomes. There is the additional problem, however, seen most clearly in the Fiorina and Plott results: the predicted chaos is not observed in controlled experiments. This finding is problematic because it suggests the possible existence of errors in the basic spatial theory. However, to date, the experimental results have not been accepted as sufficient to discredit the theory. This is partly because there have been relatively few experimental tests of the theory and partly because it is possible that some auxiliary hypotheses may exist which will allow the results to be explained within the context of the theory. More significantly, it has been the apparent lack of agreement between the theory and the empirical evidence from real legislatures which has generated the most interest and has stimulated most of the work to extend the theory. As noted above, this work has both provided several theoretical explanations for the apparent stability of real legislative outcomes and has allowed the theory to explain additional aspects of legislative decision making.

5

THE RETURN TO EQUILIBRIUM
Controlling Legislative Agendas

■ ■ ■ ■ ■

The spatial theory of simple majority rule in a multidimensional issue space implies that the chaotic disequilibrium situations described in the previous chapter are a common occurrence. As noted, however, this creates an empirical puzzle because in most real-world decision-making situations, neither chaos nor disequilibrium is frequently observed. Although there may be some unperceived chaotic and disequilibrium situations, decision-making institutions like Congress do not usually appear to wander randomly through issue spaces, nor are decisions, once made, easily overturned. Experimental outcomes in largely unstructured cases also do not appear to be randomly scattered across the issue space. This lack of agreement between theory and practice has led to attempts to explain why there is so much stability in real-world decision processes (see, e.g., Tullock 1981). Short of assuming that all decisions are made in a unidimensional space in which Black's theorem produces an equilibrium at the median, three kinds of answers to this question are possible. (1) One singles out a set of decision makers and gives them special powers to manipulate the agenda of the legislative process. (2) Simple majority rule is replaced by a form of restricted majority rule in which a set of institutional structures and rules restricts the possible outcomes and simultaneously induces stability in decision-making processes. (3) One can replace the assumption of sincere voting with a form of sophisticated voting over fixed or anticipated agendas.

In this chapter, the first of these answers will be explored. In particular, it will be shown that the existence of agenda control can induce stability in legislative decision making. However, there is a price for this method because, as will be seen, the existence of agenda control can substantially benefit those having such control at the expense of other legislators.

Agenda Control Theories

One possible way of explaining the empirical regularities of the legislative process in Congress and similar legislatures is that a particular legislator or set of legislators has control of the agenda. Those having such control can dictate which alternatives are considered and in which order. As an example of how this can work, consider again the classic paradox of voting in which there is a three-person legislature with the legislators having the following preference orders for outcomes X, Y, and Z:

$$\text{Legislator A:} \quad X > Y > Z$$
$$\text{Legislator B:} \quad Y > Z > X$$
$$\text{Legislator C:} \quad Z > X > Y$$

As has been seen before with this example, the social preference ordering here is intransitive with X preferred to Y, Y preferred to Z, and Z preferred to X. However, if legislator A has agenda control, he or she can arrange for an order of voting in which the first vote is between Y and Z so that Y wins and eliminates the only outcome that can defeat X. The second vote will then be between Y and X, and X will win, which is legislator A's most preferred outcome.[1]

Alternatively, consider the same case with legislator B rather than A having agenda control. B's most preferred outcome is Y, and from the preference orders, he or she can see that Y can defeat Z and Z can defeat X. By setting up an agenda in which the first vote is between X and Z, Z will win and eliminate X so that on the second vote, Y will defeat Z and become the social choice. Thus, both legislators A and B were able to manipulate the agenda so that their most preferred outcome became the social choice; it can also be seen that legislator C could manipulate the agenda to yield Z as the social choice.

In the examples above, the legislator with agenda control was able to exploit the fact that the social preference order was intransitive. Consider now the case in which the three legislators have the following preference orders:

Legislator A: $X > Y > Z$
Legislator B: $Y > X > Z$
Legislator C: $Z > Y > X$

It can be seen here that the social preference order is $Y > X > Z$, which is transitive, and Y is the Condorcet winning alternative. It can also be seen that there is no way to structure an agenda to prevent Y from being the outcome.[2] Y will defeat whatever alternative it is put against; so in this case, agenda control cannot be used to manipulate the outcome.

In the examples above, there was only a discrete set of alternatives, and each was required to enter the voting at some stage. Theoretically, however, spatial models of legislative decision making allow for a potentially infinite number of alternatives, and not all of them are required to enter the decision-making process. In this more general context, can agenda control be used to manipulate outcomes?

Consider first the case in which there is a unidimensional issue space, and all the legislators have single-peaked preferences. An example of such a case for a three-person legislature is given in Figure 5.1. It can be seen in this figure that the median preference peak is defined by the preference curve of legislator B so that the point labeled M is the Condorcet winning alternative. This implies that M can defeat any of the other alternatives; for this reason, if M enters the agenda at any stage, it will be the outcome. However, will M enter the agenda if one of the legislators has agenda control?

Before answering this question, an important question of legislative procedure must be addressed. In the cases in which there were only a relatively few discrete alternatives and each was required to enter the agenda, the issue of how the decision-making process ends did not arise because it was implicit that it did so when all the alternatives had entered the agenda. In the current case, however, in

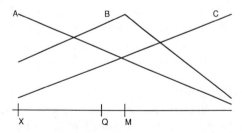

Figure 5.1.   Agenda Control in the Case of Three Legislators with Single-Peaked Preferences in a Unidimensional Issue Space

which there is a potentially infinite number of alternatives and not all of them must enter the agenda, it is unclear at what point the decision process ends and an outcome is chosen.

Real legislatures like Congress deal with this problem in two ways. First, only a fixed number of alternatives can be proposed. Thus, as seen earlier, the House allows only five alternatives: an original bill, an amendment to this bill, an amendment to the amendment, a substitute amendment, and an amendment to the substitute.[3] Alternatively, legislative rules allow for a call of the previous question which, if adopted, prohibits the offering of additional alternatives.

Because the latter of these two rules is somewhat less restrictive of the power of an agenda setter than is the former, it will be assumed in the following examples that the legislator with monopoly agenda control also has the exclusive right to call the previous question and end the decision-making process. With this rule, the decision-making process operates in the following way. The agenda setter offers an initial alternative that is immediately put against the implicit status quo motion.[4] Whichever of these wins on this first vote then becomes the extant status quo, and further alternatives can then be proposed until the previous question is moved and adopted. The last adopted motion then becomes the outcome.

Consider now the case in Figure 5.1 in which legislator A has monopoly control of the agenda. This legislator would most prefer the outcome X, where his or her preference curve has its peak. However, under the rules, the first vote must be between the implicit status quo Q and an alternative that A proposes. If legislator A proposes X, it will lose on the first vote to Q because a majority of preference curves rises toward Q in the $X–Q$ interval. More generally, it can be seen that Q will defeat any alternative located to its left, so the only alternatives that can defeat Q are those located to its right.[5] However, only the agenda setter can propose alternatives, and legislator A prefers Q to any of the alternatives to its right. Thus, in this case, Q must be the final outcome.

The fact that Q is the final outcome in this case is significant because it is not the Condorcet winner. By exploiting agenda control, legislator A was able to prevent the adoption of M, which would otherwise have been selected. This implies that when agenda control exists in a unidimensional issue space, Condorcet winning alternatives may not be adopted.

Consider now the case illustrated in Figure 5.2, which is identical to that in Figure 5.1 except that the location of Q has been altered. Again, it can be seen that legislator A's most preferred alternative

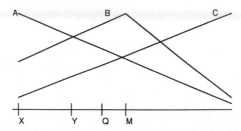

Figure 5.2. Agenda Control in the Case of Three Legislators with Single-Peaked
Preferences in a Unidimensional Issue Space

X cannot be selected because a majority of B and C prefers Q to X. It can also be seen that a majority of A and B prefers outcomes to the left of Q, and if A proposes one of these, it will defeat Q. In fact, A would have an incentive to propose the left-most alternative that can defeat Q in order to get an outcome as close to his or her most preferred outcome. Thus, in the case of Figure 5.2, agenda setter A would have an incentive to propose the alternative Y, which is just slightly preferred by legislator B to Q. Legislators A and B will then vote for Y against Q, after which A will call the previous question. It will also pass, making Y the outcome.

Again, in this case, it can be seen that agenda control by a legislator has resulted in an outcome different from the Condorcet winner. More generally, it is straightforward to show that the only times the Condorcet alternative will be chosen are when the legislator with the median preference peak has agenda control or when the positions labeled M and Y coincide. A priori for a relatively large legislature, the probability of either of these conditions existing is relatively small so that in realistic cases, it is unlikely that a Condorcet winning outcome, if one exists, will be selected.

As a final unidimensional example, consider the case illustrated in Figure 5.3. In contrast to the cases above in which all the preference curves were single peaked, the preferences in Figure 5.3 are such that they cannot simultaneously be represented by single-peaked curves.[6] Consequently, a Condorcet winning alternative does not exist in this case. Thus, the alternative M, which is under the median preference peak, cannot defeat all other alternatives, and in particular, it cannot defeat any position to the left of itself because two preference curves are rising as one moves left of M.

As in the earlier examples, assume that legislator A has agenda control. Under the procedural rules used earlier, the first motion that A makes will be put against the status quo motion Q. For legislator

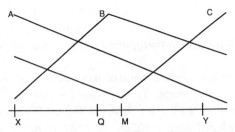

Figure 5.3. Agenda Control in the Case of Three Legislators with
Non–Single-Peaked Preferences in a Unidimensional Issue Space

A, getting his or her most preferred outcome in this case is simple.
By noting that two of the preference curves are rising toward X in
the Q–X interval, A knows that by proposing X, it will defeat Q. If
A then proposes the previous question so that no additional alter-
natives can be considered, it will also pass with the support of A and
B so that X will become the final outcome.

In the case above, legislator A was able to exploit agenda control
to achieve his or her most preferred outcome in a single step. However, this is not always possible when an intransitive social preference
order exists. For example, if legislator B in Figure 5.3 had been the
agenda controller instead of A, B could not have achieved outcome
M by simply proposing it because both A and C prefer Q to M.
Notice, however, that a majority of A and C prefers X to M, a
majority of C and B prefers Y to X, and a majority of B and A
prefers M to Y. Thus, B could first propose X, then Y, and finally
M. Each of these alternatives defeats the previous motion; if B then
calls the previous question, the final outcome will be M, B's most
preferred outcome.

The previous two examples illustrate how an agenda controller, in
a case of intransitive social preferences, was able to exploit this power
to achieve his or her most preferred outcome. It should be noted,
however, that it does not follow that an agenda controller can always
do this in the unidimensional situation. One instance of this is when
there is a cycle among a set of alternatives, including Q, and when
any of the alternatives in this cycle defeats all others. For example,
if there is a cycle among alternatives R, Q, and S such that $R >
Q > S > R$ and each of these three alternatives defeats all others,
an agenda setter cannot achieve his or her most preferred outcome
if it is not one of the three in the cycle.

Thus, the existence of agenda control in a case of socially intransitive unidimensional preferences does not imply that the controller's

most preferred outcome is selected. As the examples here have also shown, however, agenda control is a significant power that allows the legislator having it to manipulate outcomes to his or her advantage.

Up to this point, agenda control has been considered only in a unidimensional issue space. To see what happens in a multidimensional space, consider Figure 5.4. As in the earlier examples, this is a three-person legislature deciding on a two-dimensional issue. The ideal points of the three legislators are labeled with letters *A* through *C*, and it is assumed that they have circular indifference curves. As is typical of multidimensional decision making, it can be seen in the figure that social preference order is intransitive so that no equilibrium (or Condorcet outcome) exists. Here, the question is which alternative will be selected if one of the legislators has monopoly control of the agenda.

In examining this question, it is assumed that the legislature operates under the same procedural rules as above with the agenda setter having the exclusive right to call the previous question. Further, it is again assumed here that legislator A has agenda control. The questions then, are what is the extent to which A can use agenda control to manipulate outcomes, and, in particular, can A achieve an outcome corresponding to his or her ideal point?

Note first in Figure 5.4 that the status quo position *Q* will defeat A's ideal point. In fact, any alternative in the shaded area is preferred by a majority to alternative *A*. Thus, legislator A cannot propose any of these and achieve alternative *A*. However, note that the alternatives corresponding to B's ideal point would lose to A's ideal point. Also note that legislator A prefers *B* to *Q* (shown by the dashed

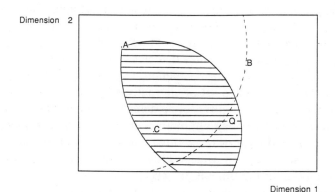

Figure 5.4. Agenda Control in a Two-Dimensional Issue Space

indifference curve). Thus, if A first proposes alternative B, it will defeat Q. Legislator A can then propose A against B, and A will defeat B. A call of the previous question will then pass (with A and C supporting it), and the final outcome will be A's ideal point.

In the case of a multidimensional issue space, this result is not extraordinary. In fact, this example is typical of all multidimensional cases in which a Plott equilibrium does not exist (McKelvey 1976, 1979). What McKelvey proved is that a monopoly agenda setter in a multidimensional issue space can manipulate the agenda to produce any outcome in the whole issue space. In some cases, this may require a relatively long agenda, but that does not detract from the fact that when a Plott equilibrium does not exist, a monopoly agenda setter can always achieve his or her ideal point as the outcome.[7]

A major implication of both the unidimensional and multidimensional examples of agenda control is that the existence of such control generally appears to make a majority of legislators worse off than they would have been in the absence of such control. Thus, in the unidimensional cases in which a Condorcet winning alternative existed, the fact that this alternative was not the final outcome implies that a majority would have achieved more utility if agenda control had not existed and the Condorcet alternative had been chosen. Similarly, a majority of B and C in Figure 5.4 would have preferred any outcome in the shaded area, including Q, to the outcome legislator A was able to achieve using agenda control.

The fact that majorities of legislators are generally made worse off by the existence of agenda control raises the serious question of why they would allow such control to exist (Riker 1980). Agenda control imposed on a legislature from the outside (e.g., by a constitution) would not make this an important problem, but generally such an imposition is not made. The U.S. Constitution, for example, explicitly states that the chambers of Congress have the right to establish their own procedural rules. From this it would follow that formal agenda control derived from legislative rules would exist either in very limited forms or not at all.

With one major exception, there is empirical support in Congress for Riker's conclusion that legislators have little incentive to grant agenda control to either individuals or groups. The exception to this conclusion is the gatekeeping power of congressional committees which allows them to prevent legislation from being considered by their full chambers. The other two instances of agenda control in Congress are the closed rule in the House, which prohibits amendments to committee bills, and the closed rule for bills reported by a conference committee. As will be shown below, neither of these appears to be a significant form of agenda control.

Consider first the gatekeeping power of congressional committees. In both the House and Senate, all bills, when introduced, are immediately referred to a standing committee for initial consideration.[8] For most bills, this is the end of their sojourn through the legislative process because committees generally do not consider most of the bills referred to them. In the 99th Congress (1985–86), for example, there were 5743 bills introduced and referred to committee in the House, but only 599 were eventually considered and reported by House committees.[9] Thus, during this congress, committees effectively killed 90 percent of the bills referred to them.

There are rules in both the House and Senate which allow the full chamber to discharge a committee from consideration of a bill so that it can be considered by the full chamber.[10] Such rules are seldom invoked, however, and even when they are, it is unlikely that the bill will become a law. In fact, as Krehbiel (1985) has shown, between 1910 and 1984, House committees were only discharged of 26 bills, and of these, only 20 became public law.

The facts that all bills are initially referred to a committee and that committees are seldom discharged from their consideration of a bill are potentially substantial forms of agenda control. In theoretical terms, however, it is unclear why such powers would be granted (Riker 1980). It should be noted that since committees fail to report 90 percent of the bills sent to them, their gatekeeping power is vastly overstated. Many of the unreported bills are duplicates of other bills, and many more would not receive majority support in the full chamber if they were reported. In addition, a full chamber majority always has the option of discharging a committee if the members of the majority really want to act on a bill. Therefore, although the existence of gatekeeping must be considered an exception to Riker's conclusion, it is not too significant an exception because many of the instances in which it is used are consistent with the preferences of full chamber majorities who have the option of discharging a committee.

Note also that committee gatekeeping is a negative power: it only allows committees to prevent the passage of bills that a committee majority prefers not to pass. As such, gatekeeping cannot explain the apparent success of committees in having their reported bills passed by their full chambers in largely unaltered form. Generally, about 90 percent of reported bills are eventually passed by the full chamber, and many of those that do not pass die not from outright rejection but from the lack of time, as they are pending action at the time Congress adjourns.[11] Moreover, the floor seldom makes any major change in reported bills. Amendments to bills in the full chamber are generally minor ones that do not substantially alter the main provisions of the bill as reported from committee.[12] If an agenda control is to be a valid explanation for the stability and general predictability of legislative decision making, it must also explain these apparent empirical instances in Congress.

One form of agenda control which would explain the success of committees in Congress is the closed rule prohibiting amendments to a bill reported from a committee. In this case, the committee reporting a bill has complete agenda control. With a closed rule, the full chamber is faced with a choice between only two alternatives: the reported bill and the status quo.

For several reasons, it does not appear that closed rules for committee bills can explain the empirical regularities observed in Congress. First, closed rules are only possible in the House so they cannot explain the success of Senate committees. Moreover, Fleisher and Bond (1981) have shown that the success of House and Senate committees in their respective chambers is nearly identical. Moreover, closed rules are seldom used in the House. In the 97th and 98th Congresses (1981–82 and 1983–84), for example, no closed rules were issued, and in the 99th Congress (1985–86), only one was issued.[13] Modified open and modified closed rules also restrict amendments and are more commonly used, but again their use cannot generally explain committee success in the Senate, which has no such rules.[14] It would thus appear that the use of formal amendment control regulations like the closed rule cannot explain the empirical regularities observed in Congress.

An alternative form of agenda control in Congress is the closed rule on bills reported from a conference committee. Shepsle and Weingast (1987) have argued that this form of agenda control explains the apparent success of congressional committees in getting their recommendations adopted by the full Congress. Calling the prohibition of amendments to conference bills *ex post* veto power, Shepsle and Weingast began their argument by noting that the membership of conference committees is made up exclusively or almost exclusively from the committees that reported the bill in each chamber. This fact along with the closed rule suggested to Shepsle and Weingast that committees can generally discard any full chamber amendment with which they disagree. For example, if a committee reports a bill B to the full chamber, and it is then amended over committee objections to B', the committee can change it back to B in conference. Further, because conference bills cannot be amended, the full chamber cannot change the bill back to B' again. Moreover, because committees have this power, there will be a reluctance on the part of full chamber legislators to push amendments opposed by the committee because even though they might win in the first round, they will lose in the last.

Although it is an interesting suggesting, there are many problems with the *ex post* veto theory as an explanation for committee power. One major problem, as Krehbiel (1987) has noted, is that the House and Senate have alternatives to conference committees for resolving their differences (see also Bach 1984). For example, a chamber can simply accept the bill as passed by the other chamber; or a chamber can amend the bill as passed by the other chamber, and send it back for either acceptance or further amendment in the other chamber. By repeating this process until a bill acceptable to both chambers is found, a conference can be avoided. Moreover, the use of such procedures is not the exception but the norm. During the 98th Congress (1983–84), for example, Krehbiel found that 86.4 percent of bills were passed with no conference; 5.4 percent were passed with some combination of a conference and rules restricting the outcome of a conference; and only 8.2 percent of differences between the chambers were resolved exclusively by a conference.

It could be argued, however, that it is not the actual occurrence of a conference but the threat of one which limits full chamber amendments. The argument is that members do not offer amendments to committee bills because they think a conference may be likely and that in the conference, the conferees from the committee will eliminate their amendment. However, what this argument ignores is that the decision of whether or not to go to conference is made by the full chamber, not by the committee. If a full chamber committee supports an amendment against the wishes of a committee majority, this same majority can also refuse to request a conference and explore alternative ways of resolving the differences between the chambers. As noted earlier, in the full chamber, a committee majority or even a unanimous committee constitutes less than 10 percent of the full membership so that any threat of a conference by this small minority need not be taken seriously. Full chambers only need send bills to conference when they feel they can trust the committee conferees to follow the wishes of a full chamber majority.

For these basic reasons, major problems exist for the *ex post* veto theory of committee power. It may explain some cases, but it cannot explain the 85 percent and more of instances in which no conference was needed. More importantly, it cannot explain the key situation in which the preferences of a committee majority are different from the preferences of a full chamber majority because it is the latter, not the former, which decides which bills go to conference.

In these three instances of congressional agenda control, the ability to affect the agenda was derived from formal rules. Thus, committee gatekeeping, the closed rule in the House, and the closed rule for conference bills are all powers granted by the rules of the House and/ or Senate. Moreover, consistent with Riker's conclusion that legislators would have little incentive to grant agenda control powers, these formal grants, with the exception of committee gatekeeping, do not appear to be very important, and they cannot explain committee success in Congress. Nevertheless, that formal agenda control does not exist as a significant power in most cases does not imply that some other form of agenda control may exist which will explain both the stability of congressional outcomes and the success of congressional committees.

One form that informal agenda control can take has been examined by Romer and Rosenthal (1978), Mackay and Weaver (1978, 1981, 1983), and Denzau and Mackay (1980). In this form, agenda control derives from a "political failure in the agenda formation process" (Mackay and Weaver 1978, 182) induced by the costs of formulating and proposing alternatives. Some costs, for example, are entailed in calculating what the content of an agenda alternative should be, drafting the alternative, and then constructing arguments to convince others why they should support the new proposal. In a congressional context, this argument suggests that committees are successful in the full chamber because of the costs involved in formulating and passing alternatives to proposed committee bills. As Fenno (1966, 1973) noted, when a congressional committee brings a bill to the full chamber, the floor managers of the bill can and generally do make a strong case that the committee members have worked hard and extensively studied the issues involved. From this work and from the knowledge they have gained, the committee members argue that they have put together a legislative package that the nonexperts in the rest of the chamber should not only support[15] but also not change by offering amendments. Such amendments, the committee will argue, are not derived from the knowledge and expertise available to the committee and therefore may have unknown or unanticipated consequences that will interfere with, or even totally thwart, the basic purpose of the legislation.

As used by congressional committees, this is a normative argument implying that noncommittee members *should* not offer amendments to committee bills. However, committees do not need to rely solely upon such a norm because if the norm is violated, committees often have available extensive facts and other data to construct a strong case against the adoption of any proposed amendment. To combat these arguments, amendment proposers need to construct alternative arguments that often require an independent set of facts. As a consequence, offering a potentially successful amendment is not a costless task; beyond the activities of formulating, drafting, and proposing an amendment, it also must be supported by argument and data. The formulation of arguments and the acquisition of relevant data, however, can be difficult, expensive, and time consuming. By thus raising the costs of proposing amendments, congressional committees attempt to discourage them, and to the extent that they are successful in limiting the number of alternatives considered, they can control the full chamber agenda and thereby win the unamended passage of their bills.

As stated, this argument implies that congressional committees have a significant amount of proposal power because of their ability to control the decision-making agenda. Moreover, as Mackay and Weaver and others have noted, this control derives from the induced costs of formulating and proposing alternatives. In these terms, the earlier noted success of congressional committees in having their bills passed in the full chamber is not a function of any formal rules but rather of informal mechanisms exploited by committees—in particular here, their expertise and informational advantages.

Note as well that a similar kind of argument can be made to explain the gatekeeping power of congressional committees. If committees are the main repository of knowledge and expertise in a policy area, the normative argument would be that committees should not be discharged of their consideration of a bill because to do so may result in the passage of a seriously flawed law. However, committees also have the resources to construct strong arguments against their being discharged, and, as above, this raises the costs for those who might propose a discharge petition. Consequently, relatively few discharge petitions would be expected, and the gatekeeping power of congressional committees would seldom be challenged.

Is such an agenda control explanation based upon the costs of formulating alternatives valid for the proposal and gatekeeping power of congressional committees? From close observers of congressional committees like Fenno (1966, 1973), there is some evidence that it may be so. In his analysis of the House Appropriations Committee, Fenno (1966, 440–41) noted that "Subcommittee spokesmen defend their recommendations on the grounds that the subcommittee specialists have a more informed understanding of the subject matter than anyone else. On this basis, they appeal for a vote of confidence from their fellow Members."

Similarly, Fleisher and Bond (1981) have shown that the single most significant factor explaining the success or failure of amendments to committee bills in both chambers of Congress was the unity of the committee. When committees were united in either support of or opposition to a proposed amendment, the committee position won almost every time; however, when there was division on the committee, the position consistent with that of a committee majority was much less likely to prevail. In the terms used above, this suggests that when the self-proclaimed committee experts are in agreement they win; but when there is disagreement among them, it is less likely that any of them will carry the full chamber.

Also consistent with the costs-of-amendments explanation of congressional committee success are the results presented by Smith (1987). He looked at amending activity in the House between 1955 and 1986 and found that although the members of any given committee constitute less than 10 percent of the membership of the House, committee members generated about half of all floor amendments. This disproportionate offering of amendments by committee members is consistent with the costs hypothesis because if there are costs to proposing full chamber amendments in the House, presumably these would be less for committee members who have the expertise gained through participation in committee hearings and mark-up sessions and who also have access to the information generated by the committee.

These observations and data suggest that the costs-of-amendments hypothesis may have some validity in explaining both the apparent stability of congressional outcomes and the success of congressional committees in their full chambers. There is additional evidence, however, which suggests that this hypothesis may be somewhat of an artifact of a more fundamental reason for congressional committee success. As elaborated more fully in Chapter 7, the more fundamental reason for committee success appears to be that committees anticipate what outcomes a majority in the full chamber will accept and do not report bills that conflict in any serious way with these anticipations. As Kingdon (1973, 127) has noted from his case studies:

These were cases in which the committee majority took a position contrary to the wishes of the House majority and attempted to defend it on the floor. Generally speaking, their defense was unsuccessful. When the whole House membership had a well-formed attitude on a given measure, the committee position could not prevail against it.

He also noted (ibid., 129) that:

It is possible, in response to such case studies of the influence of the whole House on committee action, to reply that these are rare, isolated instances, and that the normal pattern is much different. Indeed it is. The "normal" pattern has the appearance of committee dominance, in part *because* committee members generally anticipate House reaction well enough that confrontations between House and committee are rare. On such occasions, it can be argued that the whole House has still had a profound influence on the committee action.

Committee success in Congress, in other words, does not appear to be a situation in which a committee majority forces its will on a reluctant majority in the full chamber because it is so costly for the latter to formulate, offer, and pass amendments to committee bills. Rather, it appears that committees report bills at, or close to a position favored by a full chamber majority so that the only changes generally considered in the full chamber are marginal adjustments, and the benefits derived from these adjustments will often not be worth the costs of making adjustments.

Conclusions

It has been seen in this chapter that agenda control can be a significant power that not only induces stability in legislative decision making but does so to the benefit of those exercising this power. For this reason, as Riker has noted, it is not likely that legislators will grant anyone formal control of the agenda. As seen above, it does not appear that formal regulations like the closed rule in the House or the rule prohibiting amendments to conference bills can explain the apparent stability of congressional outcomes or the success of congressional committees in their full chambers. Also, it does not appear that informal cost constraints on the offering of amendments are a basic explanation of committee success. In general, committees are not successful when they oppose full chamber majorities. When a reported bill differs significantly from a position favored by a full chamber majority, the costs of formulating, offering, and passing an amendment will not constrain this majority. As discussed in more detail in Chapter 7, in these terms, the success of committees in Congress is largely explained by the fact that committees develop expectations about what positions a full chamber majority will support and report a bill that accords with these expectations.

It would thus appear that agenda control explanations are not very successful or fundamental in accounting for the success of congressional committees or the stability of congressional outcomes. In the next chapter, some alternative hypotheses are discussed.

6

THE RETURN TO EQUILIBRIUM
Structurally Inducing Stability

■　■　■　■　■

It was seen in the previous chapter that by limiting the set of alternatives that can be considered, agenda control can induce stability in legislative decision making. In spatial terms, this is equivalent to limiting possible movements in the issue of space. Such control, however, does not appear to explain the apparent stability of congressional outcomes or the success of congressional committees in getting their recommendations adopted. Moreover, even when it exists, agenda control is only a sufficient condition for a legislative equilibrium, which implies that it is not necessary to have agenda control for legislative outcomes to be stable. As a consequence, students of legislative decision making have also examined the stability-inducing properties of several other procedural rules. As with agenda control, these other rules also operate by limiting the consideration of alternatives and in doing this, have potential for structurally inducing stability in legislative decision making.

Here, two rules will be considered which have been found to exist in real legislatures and have been shown to be theoretically capable of reducing the instability or actually inducing stability in legislative decision making. One of these is the rule concerning the order in which alternatives are considered and in particular, when the status quo motion is considered. A second rule is the division of the question rule, which requires that multidimensional issues be considered one dimension at a time.

Forward and Backward Agenda Rules

As noted several times in previous chapters, in Congress and most other legislatures, the status quo motion enters the voting process last. Thus, the last vote held always involves the question of whether a bill should be passed and become law or should not be passed and the extant status quo maintained. In the literature on legislative decision making, this is known as a *backward moving agenda process* (Shepsle and Weingast 1984a; Wilson 1986).

An alternative way of proceeding, known as a *forward moving agenda process*, is for the extant status quo motion to be considered on the first vote. In this case, the initial vote is between the existing status quo and some proposed alternative. If the status quo gets a majority on this vote, it is either the final decision, and no change in law is made, or additional motions to alter the status quo are allowed. If the status quo loses on this vote, the alternative that defeated it becomes the new status quo, and further alternatives to this new status quo can then be proposed. This process then repeats itself until a call of the previous question is made and approved or, if there is a rule limiting the number of votes that can be held (or, equivalently, the number of alternatives that can be proposed), until this limit is reached.

To see the different consequences of using a forward instead of a backward moving agenda process, consider the case presented in Figure 6.1, in which there is a two-dimensional issue space, and the ideal points of the members of a five-person legislature are labeled A through E. For the purposes of this example, it will be assumed that each legislator has separable preferences that can be represented with circular indifference curves. Further, it will be assumed that the status quo of existing law corresponds to the point labeled Q. Proceeding in the usual way by drawing the indifference curves of each legislator through Q, it can be seen that all the alternatives in the shaded areas are inside the indifference curves of three legislators and hence are preferred by a majority to Q. Now, when the status quo Q enters the voting last, as in the backward moving agenda process, the only possible outcomes are Q and those corresponding to the points in the shaded areas which are majority preferred to Q. If the alternative matched against Q on this last vote is not in the shaded area, Q will win; any of the alternatives in the shaded areas will defeat Q. An important consequence of this situation is that with a backward moving agenda process, Q can act as a limit on the possible outcomes, preventing the legislative process from producing outcomes anywhere in the issue space.

Alternatively, consider what happens in Figure 6.1 when a forward moving agenda process is used. With Q entering on the first vote, it can once again be seen that the only alternatives that can defeat Q are those in the shaded areas. Assume that one of these is proposed and defeats Q. This alternative becomes the new status quo, and the process is repeated. However, as was seen in Chapter 4, in a multidimensional issue space, this new status quo is vulnerable to a new set of alternatives and, in particular, to those inside the three indifference curves drawn through this new Q. Proposing one of these will defeat the new Q and replace it as the status quo. As was seen earlier, however, for any point in the issue space, it will generally be possible to find a set of points that will defeat it; this implies that if there is no limit on the number of votes or alternatives, the process may wander anywhere in the issue space. Some alternative will always be majority preferred to an existing status quo, and from McKelvey (1976) it is known that any alternative in the issue space can, at least temporarily, be an outcome. This is not possible, however, with a backward moving agenda process because only those alternatives that are majority preferred to the original status quo can be outcomes.

What is particularly interesting about forward and backward moving agenda processes is that in Congress and other real legislatures, the backward moving process is always used, whereas most of the theoretical literature on legislative decision making assumes a forward moving agenda process. Moreover, as the example in Figure 6.1 made clear, the consequences of using one of these rather than the other

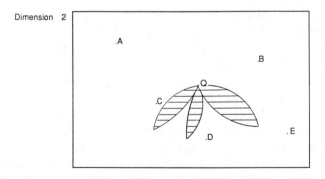

Figure 6.1.   With a Forward Moving Agenda Process, the Alternatives That Can Defeat the Initial Status Quo (Q)

are very different. A forward moving agenda process can theoretically produce outcomes from anywhere in the issue space. Such a process is considerably more chaotic and unpredictable than a backward moving process in which the outcomes are limited to those alternatives that can defeat the original status quo. A backward moving process is not sufficient to establish a unique legislative equilibrium, but it can severely reduce the possible outcomes, often to those in the neighborhood of the original status quo. As a consequence, the theoretical predictions that legislative decision making in Congress and similar legislatures is chaotic and unpredictable are not entirely wrong. However, because these theories are based upon an empirically inappropriate assumption about the agenda process, they greatly overstate the scope of the chaos in real legislatures. With a backward moving agenda process, the range of possible outcomes will be limited to the status quo and those outcomes that can defeat the status quo. A further consequence of this is that if their theories are intended to have empirical validity, theorists should concentrate their attentions on backward moving agenda processes.

To someone familiar with the history of the literature on decision making, outcomes like those in Figure 6.1, in which the only possible outcomes with a backward moving agenda process are relatively close to Q, look suspiciously like those predicted by the theory of incrementalism (Braybrook and Lindblom 1962; Lindblom 1965; Wildavsky 1964). According to the theory of incrementalism, decision making in institutions like Congress will take the existing status quo as given and then make relatively minor adjustments to it. In these terms, new outcomes will look very much like the original status quo with some minor variations.

The resemblance between incrementalism and the rational/spatial theory, however, is only superficial. In addition to the fact that these two theories originate in different intellectual traditions, the predictions derived from them can be very different. Thus, the fact that the possible outcomes in Figure 6.1 are relatively close to Q is an artifact of the location of Q with respect to the ideal points of the five legislators. In Figure 6.1, Q is located near the geometric center of the ideal points; whenever this is the case, the overlap of a majority of indifference curves will be relatively small, and the region defined by these overlapping curves will generally be close to Q. As a result, the alternatives that defeat Q will be located relatively near Q. Alternatively, when Q is located far from the center of the ideal points, as in Figure 6.2, the areas at which a majority of indifference curves overlap are considerably larger as is the distance of many of these feasible outcomes from Q. In this case, changes that depart significantly and not incrementally from Q are possible.

Figure 6.2 also illustrates a situation in which a backward moving agenda rule is not a very important constraint on possible outcomes because in this case, very few outcomes are excluded. One implication of this situation is that the degree to which a backward moving agenda rule reduces the chaos and unpredictability of legislative decision making will vary with the location of the status quo position relative to the location of the ideal points of the legislators. In general, the further the status quo is from the geometric center of the ideal points, the greater the number of possible outcomes and thus the greater the potential unpredictability of the outcome.

A second implication follows for continuing legislatures that periodically reconsider the same issues. If the continuing members of such legislatures do not alter the position of their ideal points very much over time, and the ideal points of new members do not differ much from the location of those they replace, the distribution of ideal points can be expected to change only gradually over time. Also, the status quo position is the position that was adopted by a majority the last time the same set of issues was considered; for reasons considered later in this chapter and in Chapter 7, there is reason to expect that at the time it was adopted, the current status quo was located at or near the center of the ideal points of the legislators. Together, slow changing ideal points and a status quo near the center of the ideal points imply, as seen in Figure 6.1, that a backward moving agenda rule will drastically limit the possible changes that can be made in the status quo to those in the shaded areas near the extant status quo position. Thus, in this case, a backward moving agenda rule is an

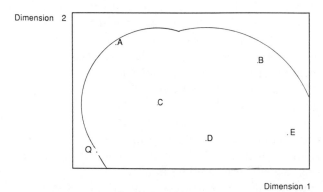

Figure 6.2.   Set of Alternatives That Defeat the Status Quo (Q)

important limiter of possible outcomes, and further, the outcomes that are possible may look like they are only marginal or incremental changes from existing policy although for reasons different from those suggested by the theory of incremental decision making.

Note also that the status quo being the last motion to enter the voting process does not necessarily give it a special theoretical advantage.[1] As is known from McKelvey's theorem and illustrated in Figure 6.1, for the outcome corresponding to any given point in the issue space, there will generally be another set of possible outcomes that can defeat it. In particular, on the last vote, there will be a set of outcomes that can defeat the status quo. Thus, in this sense, the process is not necessarily biased in favor of existing law. Further, as was seen in Figure 6.2, the alternatives that defeat the status quo do not necessarily need to involve only incremental changes. At the same time, although a backward moving agenda process does not advantage the status quo motion, the requirement that the status quo motion enter last does restrict the possible outcomes that can be passed. In doing this, the status quo motion, although not advantaged itself, does bias the process in favor of a select set of outcomes. In particular, the advantaged outcomes are those preferred by a majority to the status quo, so that one consequence of a legislature using a backward moving agenda process is that no change in law will be made except one preferred by a majority to the status quo. With the alternative forward moving agenda process, this is not always the case because by eliminating the status quo on the first vote, outcomes that are not majority preferred to existing law can win and become new law.

It should also be noted that the way in which a backward moving agenda process operates to restrict possible outcomes holds for cases in which legislators adopt sincere strategies and vote their true preferences as well as for cases in which they adopt sophisticated strategies. As was noted in Chapter 3, on the last vote, both sincere and sophisticated voters always vote sincerely. However, here, with a backward moving agenda process, this means that the final vote will be between the status quo motion and some proposed alternative, and on this vote, only the status quo and outcomes sincerely preferred to it can win.

This does not imply, however, that the outcome with sincere and sophisticated legislators will be the same. One major difference is the likelihood that the extant status quo will win. Sincere legislators myopically vote their true preferences without anticipating outcomes on later votes. In particular, sincere legislators either do not know which set of outcomes can defeat the status quo or, if they do know, vote as if they did not know. It follows that in choosing a position to put against the status quo on the last vote, sincere voting legislators may choose a position that cannot defeat the status quo, and the *à priori* likelihood of this happening will be larger as the size of the set of outcomes that defeat the status quo gets smaller. On the other hand, sophisticated voting legislators know the ideal points of the other legislators and can calculate which positions defeat the status quo. A majority that prefers a change in the status quo can thus adopt strategies so that the last vote will be between the status quo and a position that defeats it. It thus follows that sincere voting legislators are much more likely to adopt the status quo position than are sophisticated voting legislators.

More generally, it appears that one reason outcomes in real legislatures are not as chaotic and unpredictable as suggested by theory is that real legislatures use a backward moving agenda process. By restricting possible outcomes to the status quo and motions that are sincerely preferred by a majority to it, such an agenda process reduces the set of possible outcomes and in doing this, limits the range of possible outcomes that theory suggests would otherwise exist. Moreover, it was seen that this limitation is most important for continuing legislatures that periodically reconsider the same issues and do not have a fast turnover of members. It was also seen, however, that the existence of such a process is only a limit on possible outcomes and is not sufficient by itself to establish a unique equilibrium outcome.

Division of the Question Rules

As seen in the previous section, a backward moving agenda process can limit the possible outcomes of legislative decision making, but such a rule is not sufficient to establish a unique legislative equilibrium. A rule that in some cases can establish such an equilibrium is a division of the question rule (Kadane 1972). As stated in the rules of the House, a division of the question rule allows that "On the demand of any Member, before the question is put, a question shall be divided if it includes propositions so distinct in substance that one being taken away a substantive proposition shall remain" (Rule 16, clause 6). Similar rules exist in the Senate (Rule 15, clause 3) and in *Robert's Rules of Order.*

In spatial terms, what a division of the question rule does is require decision making to proceed one dimension at a time. Along with the important assumption that all the legislators have separable preferences, it can be shown that such a rule is sufficient to guarantee a stable equilibrium at the median in each dimension (Kramer 1972).[2] This result is illustrated in Figure 6.3. Without a division of the question rule and all legislators adopting sincere voting strategies, the position X is not an equilibrium because a majority prefers to X all the bills corresponding to points in the shaded areas. Moreover, all these positions could be reached because amendments simultaneously changing the positions on both dimensions are possible. With a division of the question rule, however, this is no longer possible. Only moves on one dimension at a time are allowed. Thus, if dimension 1 is considered first, only horizontal moves are possible. Now consider that the starting point is Y, a point in one of the shaded areas, which was previously seen to be able to defeat X (with the support of legislators A, C, and D). Ignoring the second dimension, it can be seen that the median preference peak corresponds to the location of D.[3] Thus, the starting point Y is to the left of the median through D, and a motion to move right on this dimension to the median position D on this dimension (i.e., to move to the point labeled Z) will get the support of legislators B, D, and E. Moreover, note that Z, being on the median in the first dimension, cannot be defeated by any other motion because D will oppose all such changes, and A and C opposing movement to the right, and B and E opposing any movement to the left. Thus, given sincere voting and the starting point of Y, Z is a stable equilibrium on dimension 1.

With a division of the question rule, after moving to Z, the legislature would then consider movements on dimension 2. In Figure 6.3, it can be seen that the median preference peak on dimension 2 corresponds to the location of C, and Z is below this median. Thus,

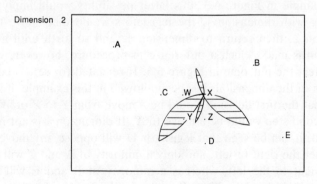

Figure 6.3. Division of the Question Rule with Separable Preferences Allows a Stable Equilibrium to Exist

a majority consisting of A, B, and C would support moving up from
Z to X. C would then oppose any other movement on dimension 2,
with A and B opposing any downward movement, and D and E
opposing any upward movement. Thus, starting from point Z, X is
a stable equilibrium in dimension 2.

It can also be seen in Figure 6.3 that the order in which the dimensions are considered does not affect the final outcome.[4] Assuming
sincere voting and considering dimension 2 first, it can be seen that
Y, like Z, is below the median position on the second dimension,
and a majority of A, B, and C would favor a move upward to the
median (labeled W in the figure). Also, no other position on this
dimension could get a majority against W because C would oppose
all other motions, D and E would oppose all upward movements,
and A and B would oppose all downward movements. Thus, starting
with dimension 2, the outcome would first move to W, and by a
similar argument, it would then move to the median on dimension 1
so that again, the final outcome would be X. Thus, in this case, which
is representative of all cases in which the legislators have separable
preferences and vote sincerely, a division of the question rule is
sufficient to induce a stable equilibrium that is not affected by the
order in which the dimensions are considered (or the point from which
the process starts).

In the case considered here, it was assumed that with two dimensions, the legislators made only two decisions, one on each dimension.
However, as Ordeshook (1986) has noted, this is not the only form
of issue-by-issue voting that could be imposed by a division of the
question rule. A different possibility would be one in which the legislators repeatedly alternate between (or among) the dimensions.[5] In
the example in Figure 6.3, this latter possibility would imply that,
starting with dimension 1, the legislators would then move to dimension 2, then return to dimension 1, and so forth until a final
decision is made. Such a difference in procedure, however, would
not affect the outcome in Figure 6.3. If repeated (or serial) consideration of the dimensions has been allowed in this example, it is still
true that the first decision would be a move from Y to Z or W, and
the second step would be a move to X. If dimension 1 is not reconsidered, it can be seen that legislator D will oppose any movement
to either the right or left, and only a minority of A and C will favor
movement to the left, whereas a minority of B and E will favor
movement to the right. Thus X cannot be defeated and is thus stable
under the rule.

In the cases considered above, it was assumed that legislators had separable preferences and voted sincerely. It can also be shown that a stable equilibrium at the median of each dimension exists for sophisticated legislators who have separable preferences (Kramer 1972; see also Denzau and Mackay 1981). This latter case can be analyzed using the decision tree in Figure 6.4. Assume in Figure 6.4 that the position of X_1 corresponds to the median on dimension 1 and that Y_1 corresponds to the median on dimension 2. It is straightforward to show that if the first decision (on dimension 1) is X_1, the second decision (on dimension 2) will be Y_1. Thus, with an odd number of voters, one legislator's ideal point will correspond to Y_1, and this legislator will oppose movement either upward or downward on dimension 2. Further, because Y_1 is the median, ideal points, one short of a majority, are located above Y_1 and the same number below. Hence, with the support of the legislator whose ideal point is at Y_1, movement neither upward nor downward is possible, and so Y_1 must defeat Y_2 regardless of the position Y_2 represents. Thus, on both the left and right branches in Figure 6.4, the sophisticated equivalent of the second decision is Y_1.

With Y_1 being the outcome on the second dimension, the first decision can be seen to be a choice between the points (X_1, Y_1) and (X_2, Y_1). As these are equivalent on the second dimension, they only differ on X_1 and X_2. By assumption, X_1 is the median position on dimension 1, and by an analogous argument to that used above, X_1 will defeat X_2. Thus, the final outcome will be (X_1, Y_1), which is the joint median position. This outcome is the same as when all vote sincerely, and the conclusion illustrated by this example is that with separable preferences and a division of the question rule, the median in each dimension is a stable equilibrium under both sincere and sophisticated voting.

It has thus been seen that with all legislators having separable preferences, a division of the question rule is sufficient to guarantee a legislative equilibrium at the point at which lines (or planes) drawn through the median preference on each dimension intersect. In the

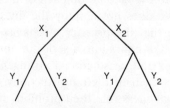

Figure 6.4. Sophisticated Voting Tree for a Division of the Question Rule

example above, it is still true that majorities of legislators in Figure 6.3 prefer alternatives to X, but the division of the question rule prevents them from reaching these positions. In this sense, a division of the question rule acts much like agenda control in limiting what alternatives can be considered, and by doing this, it forces an equilibrium to exist; as it is sometimes stated, such a rule structurally induces an equilibrium on legislative decision making.

As described above, a division of the question rule in the congressional context functions as a limitation on the content of full chamber amendments. Under this rule, amendments are either required to address a single issue (or dimension), or they will be divided into a series of amendments that address single issues. For purposes of reference, this will be called *amendment level* division of the question. This is necessary because Shepsle (1979) has presented an alternative model that can appropriately be called *committee level* division of the question.[6]

What Shepsle proposed is that decision-making processes such as those found in most legislatures contain three basic kinds of organizational arrangements that limit the potential instability of outcomes: (1) a committee system that functions as an institutionally based division of labor; (2) a jurisdictional arrangement among the committees dividing the policy space among them; and (3) an amendment control rule (called the germaneness rule) that limits the issue dimensions on which committees can make proposals. Shepsle also assumed that legislators use sincere voting strategies and a forward moving agenda process. He then showed that if committees have simple (or one-dimensional) jurisdictions, if the preference curves of legislators are single peaked in each dimension, "and if a germaneness rule [limiting amendments to only the dimension within the jurisdiction of the committee] governs the amendment process, then structure-induced equilibrium exists" (ibid., 47). Moreover, if the legislative preferences are separable so that preference rankings of points on one dimension are independent of rankings on other dimensions, then in a legislative setting the structure-induced equilibrium is the bill corresponding to the median on each of the dimensions.

Although Shepsle does not employ the division of the question concept, it is clear that the primary mechanism he uses to induce stability is a division of issues into a series of unidimensional spaces. His division of labor and jurisdictional arrangements establish committees and restrict each of their jurisdictions to a single issue dimension. His germaneness rule then prohibits full chamber amendments that violate the unidimensional jurisdiction of the committee that reported a bill. Hence, at both the committee and full chamber levels, Shepsle has reduced legislative decision making to a series of unidimensional issue spaces. Then, using Black's theorem, he shows that the outcomes of this decision-making process will correspond to the median preference peak on each of the dimensions.

Because of its ability to induce a unique equilibrium on legislative decision making, a division of the question rule is a more powerful stability-inducing rule than is the backward moving agenda process, which only limits the range of possible outcomes. Three further questions remain. First, what outcome should be expected when both a division of the question and a backward moving agenda rule are used? Second, can a division of the question rule either alone or in combination with some other rule actually explain the apparent stability of outcomes in legislatures like Congress? Finally, is a division of the question rule sufficient to induce stability when the preferences of legislators are not separable?[7]

Consider first the question concerning the use of both a backward moving agenda and division of the question rule. From the earlier analysis of backward moving agendas, it is known that such a process forces a final choice between the status quo Q and the set of outcomes that can defeat Q (or the set $W(Q)$, the win set of the status quo). A division of the question rule, on the other hand, selects the outcome corresponding to the median ideal point on each dimension. When both rules are imposed simultaneously, and legislators adopt sincere voting strategies, the division of the question rule will lead to the selection of the median position on each dimension, and then the backward moving agenda rule will cause this joint median position to be put against the status quo motion on a final vote. On this vote, the joint median position can defeat all outcomes in the issue space except those inside a majority of indifference curves through the joint median position. In Figure 6.3, for example, the joint median position X can defeat all outcomes except those corresponding to points in the shaded areas. If the status quo position is located in one of these areas, it will defeat X; otherwise, X will be the outcome. A major consequence of this is that the outcome with a division of the question rule and sincere voting will not always be the joint median position when a backward moving agenda process is used.[8] However, this does not imply instability or the selection of an arbitrary outcome because the only possible alternative to the joint median in this case is the status quo position. Moreover, as seen earlier, sincere voters do not anticipate outcomes on subsequent votes, so that in adopting the joint median position, the *à priori* probability that this will be defeated by the status quo increases as the size of the set of points that defeat the status quo decreases.

The result above assumes that legislators adopt sincere voting strategies. The alternative is that they adopt sophisticated strategies; in this case, a different conclusion from that above is warranted. To see the consequences of the use of sophisticated voting strategies, remember that on the last vote, which is a choice between the status quo position Q and some alternative, all vote sincerely. This means that the only possible outcomes are Q or outcomes in the win set of Q—that is, positions inside a majority of indifference curves drawn through Q. If the outcome at the intersection of medians is in the win set of Q, it can be shown that it is an equilibrium; the fact that a backward moving agenda process is used is of no consequence. As originally shown by Kramer (1972), sophisticated actors using a division of the question rule will choose the outcome corresponding to the median in each dimension, and the fact that a final vote between this alternative and Q is held does not alter this conclusion when a majority sincerely prefers the joint median alternative to Q.

This still leaves open the question of which alternative will be selected when a majority sincerely prefers Q to X. If X is chosen and is then put against Q on the last vote, Q will win with all voting sincerely. There are majorities, however, which prefer various outcomes to Q as is shown for the simple case of three legislators in Figure 6.5.[9] As sophisticated actors, each legislator can anticipate this situation and knows that by adopting the median on each dimension, the final outcome will be Q. However, various majorities of these legislators prefer other outcomes to Q and will attempt to devise

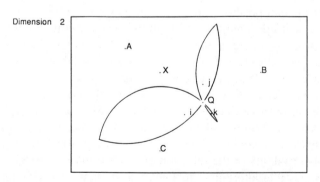

Figure 6.5. Existence of a Cycle among the Alternatives That Defeat the
Status Quo (Q)

strategies to bring about the adoption of one of them. Which one will they adopt? Unfortunately, this question does not have a definitive answer for it is easy to show in this case that a social preference cycle exists among the set of outcomes that defeat Q. In Figure 6.5, for example, let the starting point be some arbitrary outcome, and let the first decision be the adoption of some position on the horizontal line through this starting point (an equivalent case exists if the first decision is to be made on the vertical dimension). For sophisticated legislators, this is not a unidimensional decision because they also anticipate which decision will be made on the second dimension in considering the first dimension. Because of this, the decision-making process is inherently multidimensional despite the division of the question rule. Thus, in the case in Figure 6.5, the problem is to determine if there is a point in the win set of Q which defeats all other points in this set. In general, such a point will not exist. In the specific case at hand, for example, a social preference cycle exists among the points i, j, and k such that j, favored by legislators A and B, defeats i; k, favored by B and C, defeats j; and i, favored by A and C, defeats k. As a consequence, it is impossible for the three legislators to define appropriate sophisticated strategies for themselves because these strategies must be contingent upon what the other legislators are doing. Thus, in this case, no equilibrium exists, and the outcome is indeterminant.

What is especially significant about this result is that it implies that the stability-inducing properties of some rules can be nullified by other stability-inducing rules. Given that real legislatures operate with a great many procedural rules, this implies that the existence of real legislative equilibria cannot be explained by showing that a given rule is sufficient to induce stability and is used in a given legislature. Rather, to explain legislative equilibria requires the simultaneous examination of a whole constellation of procedural rules.

Consider now the second question raised earlier concerning whether or not a division of the question rule alone or in combination with a backward moving agenda rule is an adequate explanation for the apparent stability of real outcomes. Consider first what was earlier called amendment level division of the question. One very interesting case in which such a rule appears to have been implicitly used was found by Jillson and Wilson (1987). In their analysis of decision making in the Continental Congress, they did not focus explicitly on the use of a division of the question rule. However, because of the nature of the political context in 1779, with each state considered a sovereign entity and little opportunity for the delegates to trade votes across different issues, it appeared that an implicit division of the question procedure was used whereby each issue dimension was treated independently from the others. Through an extensive analysis of the roll-call votes held during 1779, Jillson and Wilson concluded that outcomes on each dimension approached the median preference peak on that dimension—a result consistent with Black's theorem if the legislators had separable preferences and if either an explicit or implicit division of the question rule were in effect.

There is less evidence, however, for a division of the question rule inducing stability in more modern times. As seen earlier, such a rule exists in both the House and Senate, but these rules do not appear to be invoked frequently.[10] Close observers of Congress like Fenno (1966, 1973), Bach (1987), and others have not noted any extensive use of such a rule. Moreover, the evidence that does exist suggests that these rules are not self-imposed either. For example, in discussing the germaneness rule in the Senate, Bach (1987) presented a case in which both nongermane and multidimensional amendments were proposed, and the division of the question rule was not invoked.

It thus appears that an amendment level division of the question rule is not an adequate explanation for the apparent stability of congressional outcomes. Similarly, Shepsle's committee level division of the question model also does not appear to be empirically valid in a congressional context. As Shepsle suggested, Congress and many other American-type legislatures have committee systems, jurisdictional arrangements, and germaneness rules for these committees. However, it is not true that these committees have only simple one-dimensional jurisdictions, nor are the bills they report unidimensional. The House Committee on Banking, Finance, and Urban Affairs, for example, has jurisdiction over "(1) Banks and banking, including deposit insurance and Federal monetary policy; (2) money and credit, including currency and the issuance of notes and redemption thereof; gold and silver, including the coinage thereof; valuations and revaluations of the dollar; (3) urban development; (4) public and private housing; (5) economic stabilization, defense production, renegotiation, and control of the price of commodities, rents, and services" and several other areas as well. This is certainly not a simple jurisdiction as defined by Shepsle; even with a germaneness rule linked to the jurisdiction of the committee, it is insufficient to produce unidimensional decision making in Congress. If Shepsle's rules do not induce unidimensional decision making, then they are also insufficient to induce an issue-by-issue equilibrium on congressional decision making.

The Problem of Nonseparable Preferences

The structure-induced equilibrium results in the previous section are based to a considerable degree on the assumption that legislators have separable preferences so that the alternatives they prefer on one dimension are independent of those they prefer on others.

As seen in Chapter 4, separable preferences can be represented either by circular indifference curves or by elliptical indifference curves in which the axes of the ellipses are parallel to those of the issue space. Like separable preferences, nonseparable ones can be represented by elliptical indifference curves; but for nonseparable preferences, the axes of these ellipses are not parallel to those of the issue space (see Figure 6.6).

To see why the term *nonseparable* is appropriate for preferences represented by nonparallel elliptical indifference curves, consider the two legislators whose indifference curves are shown in Figure 6.6. In part *A* of this figure, the separable preferences of a legislator are illustrated. For this legislator, the most preferred outcome on the Y dimension is independent of what outcome might be chosen on the X dimension. For example, this legislator most prefers Y_1 on the Y

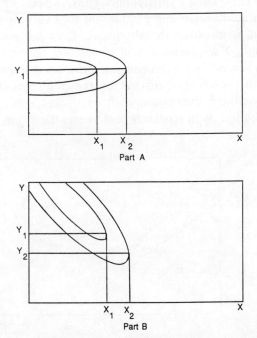

Figure 6.6. Separable and Nonseparable Preference Curves

dimension regardless of whether X_1 or X_2 is chosen on the X dimension. Consider now the legislator with nonseparable preferences, shown in part B of the figure. If this legislator thinks that X_1 will be the outcome on the X dimension, he or she will most prefer the position Y_1 on the Y dimension.[11] If the legislator thinks that the outcome on the X dimension will be X_2, he or she will most prefer Y_2 on the Y dimension. Thus, in this case, the order of preferences for outcomes on the Y dimension is contingent on, or not separable from, positions on the X dimension; looked at the other way, preference orders on the X dimension are contingent on positions on the Y dimension.

To analyze decision making when legislators do not have separable preferences, the concept of optima or ridge lines is useful (Denzau and Mackay 1981). In a two-dimensional issue space, such lines define the alternatives most preferred on one dimension for any given alternative in the other dimension. Thus, in Figure 6.7, the line $Y|X$ identifies the alternatives this legislator would prefer on the Y dimension given a position X on the X dimension. This line is drawn through the ideal point of the legislator (labeled A here) and through the left-most and right-most points of tangency between his or her indifference curves and a vertical line. Thus, the point Z is the point at which an indifference curve is tangent to a vertical line through X_1. As such, it identifies the alternative Y_1 as the most preferred outcome on the Y dimension if X_1 is the outcome on the X dimension. Similarly, a second line $X|Y$ could be constructed showing this legislator's most preferred alternative on the X dimension given any alternative on the Y dimension.

As seen earlier, with separable preferences, decisions being made

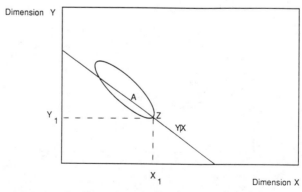

Figure 6.7. Legislator with Nonseparable Preference Curves

one issue at a time, and no backward moving agenda rule, the median outcome on each dimension would be the expected outcome. Moreover, with separable preferences, it was straightforward to locate the median position on each dimension. In previous examples, this was done by simply ignoring other dimensions and determining the location of the median ideal point on the dimension of interest. This was possible because with the axes of indifference curves parallel to those of the issue space, the order of preference for any position on a given dimension was not affected by preferences for positions on other dimensions. However, in Figure 6.6 it was seen that this is no longer true with nonseparable preferences. The legislator whose preferences are given in this figure most prefers X_1 on the X dimension if Y_1 is the outcome on the Y dimension but prefers X_2 if Y_2 is the Y dimension outcome. Thus, in this case, one cannot simply ignore the Y dimension in determining this legislator's preference order on the X dimension, nor can it be assumed, as it can with separable preferences, that his or her most preferred X dimension outcome corresponds to the location of his or her ideal point on that dimension.

One consequence of the above is that the median position on any given dimension is contingent on preferences on other dimensions. This is illustrated in Figure 6.8, in which the ideal points and optima lines of three legislators, A, B, and C, are given. Assume initially that the Y dimension outcome is fixed and corresponds to Y_1. To determine the median X dimension preference given Y_1, first draw a horizontal line through Y_1, as in the figure, and find the positions on this line which correspond to the median optima line. In doing this, it can be seen that the median tangent point corresponds to X_1. Repeat this process with the assumption that Y_2 is the fixed position on the

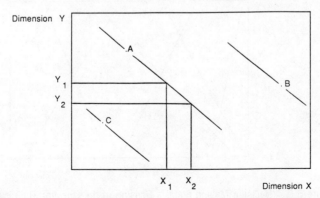

Figure 6.8.   Three Legislators with Nonseparable Preference Curves

Y dimension, and it can be seen that the median preferred position is no longer X_1 but X_2. Thus, as this simple example illustrates, the median position on a given dimension with nonseparable preferences is contingent on what position is assumed to be fixed on other dimensions.

To examine the consequences of nonseparable preferences for legislative outcomes, consider the case illustrated in Figure 6.9. In the figure, the three legislators' ideal points are labeled A, B, and C, and the optima lines for each legislator for each dimension are given. Thus, the line labeled $Y_A|X$ represents legislator A's most preferred alternatives on the Y dimension for a given alternative on the X dimension, whereas the one labeled $X_A|Y$ represents this legislator's most preferred alternatives on the X dimension for a given alternative on the Y dimension.

To analyze the decision-making process represented in this figure, consider first three optima lines $X_A|Y$, $X_B|Y$, and $X_C|Y$. It can be seen that the $X_A|Y$ line is always between the other two, implying that legislator A's preferences define the median preferred outcome on X for a given position on Y. Similarly, note that the $Y_B|X$ line is always between the $Y_A|X$ and $Y_C|X$ lines so that this line defines the median preferred outcome on Y for a given position on X.

Assume now that decision making in Figure 6.9 starts at position Q and that a division of the question rule is in effect with the first decision to be made on the X dimension. Also assume that the legislators vote sincerely and do not have foresight. Accordingly, they assume that the outcome on the other dimension will remain fixed at its present location when they are considering a given dimension.

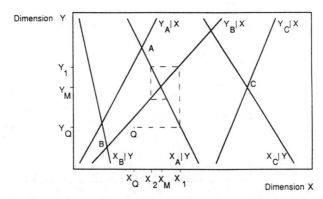

Figure 6.9.   Decision Making under a Division of the Question Rule When Legislators Do Not Have Separable Preferences

With these assumptions, a straightforward application of Black's theorem implies the existence of an equilibrium. Starting at Q, the first decision will be a horizontal move to the median preferred outcome, which is labeled X_1 in the figure. This follows because with the Y dimension assumed fixed at Y_Q, the position X_1 cannot be defeated because A most prefers this to any other outcome (given Y_Q), whereas B will oppose any movement to the right of X_1, and C will oppose any movement to the left. Thus, X_1 will be the first dimension decision, and the legislators will next consider the Y dimension.[12] In an analogous manner, with the X dimension fixed at X_1, they will proceed to adopt Y_1 corresponding to the median preference on Y given X_1. Again, considering the X dimension, they will next move to X_2 (given Y_1). Continuing to alternate between the dimensions, it can be seen that they will spiral in toward the point corresponding to X_M and Y_M at which the median lines in both dimensions intersect. Moreover, it can be seen that this position is a stable equilibrium for it cannot be defeated by any alternative possible under the division of the question rule.

Note, however, that the fact that an equilibrium exists in the case illustrated in Figure 6.9 does not imply that such an equilibrium can always be reached. To see this, consider the case illustrated in Figure 6.10 in which only the median optima lines are given. On the left, if the decision process starts at the position labeled Q_1, it can be seen that the series of outcomes will spiral in toward the M equilibrium point as in the previous example. However, on the right, it can be seen that the process does not spiral in toward the equilibrium but continually moves away from it.[13] An important consequence of this result is that the existence of an equilibrium point does not always imply that the legislative outcome will be this equilibrium position.

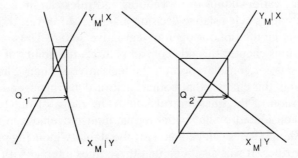

Figure 6.10.   Possible Outcomes with Decision Making under a Division of the Question Rule and Nonseparable Preferences

The results above are based in part on the assumption that the legislators did not have foresight, and therefore they could not anticipate possible outcomes on other dimensions. When this assumption is replaced with one that allows legislators to have foresight and anticipate future decisions, Denzau and Mackay showed that in general, no stable equilibrium exists. The reason is that expectations of decisions on other dimensions may induce preferences on a given dimension which are not single peaked so that Black's theorem no longer applies. Moreover, if preference curves are not single peaked, no equilibrium will exist for either sincere or sophisticated voting strategies, nor will rules like division of the question be successful in inducing an equilibrium.

From these results, it can be seen how important the assumption of separable preferences is for the existence of a multidimensional equilibrium position. When preferences are separable, it has been relatively easy to find a set of rules (e.g., division of the question) which will structurally induce a stable equilibrium on legislative decision making. However, when preferences are not separable, such rules may fail to induce an equilibrium, and even when such an equilibrium exists, it may not be possible for it to be reached.

The importance of the separability assumption naturally raises the question of whether or not real legislators can be expected to have separable preferences. Unfortunately, however, there is currently no answer to this question. Moreover, this is an empirical question, not a theoretical one, and as such, can only be resolved by empirical research.

Some Conclusions Concerning Legislative Equilibria

The basic theme of this chapter as well as the preceding one has been that various kinds of procedures and rules can induce equilibrium outcomes in legislative decision making. Moreover, they do this by restricting the options open to legislative actors. Thus, as seen in the previous chapter, agenda control restricts the ability of actors to place items for consideration on the legislative agenda. Similarly, it was seen in this chapter that both a backward moving agenda process and division of the question rules limit the range of outcomes that can be considered or, in spatial terms, limit movement in the issue space. Similar cases can be made for the stability-inducing properties of other rules. It was also seen that these rules interact with the kind of preferences legislators hold as well as the kinds of strategies legislators pursue to determine legislative outcomes. In particular, the

importance of the assumption that legislators hold separable preferences has been noted. As a general rule, it appears that when
legislators have separable preferences, rules such as division of the
question can induce stability on legislative decision making. However,
when legislators have nonseparable preferences, and especially when
they have foresight and can anticipate future decisions, no equilibrium
generally exists, and no rules may be able to induce such an equilibrium. Unfortunately, however, it is not currently known whether real
legislators generally have separable or nonseparable preferences.

7

THE RETURN TO EQUILIBRIUM
Sophisticated Voting and Uncovered Sets

■ ■ ■ ■ ■

The two preceding chapters showed a number of ways in which various procedural rules can affect the stability and predictability of legislative outcomes. It has been seen that rules like division of the question and agenda control can induce stability in legislative decision making under some conditions; and rules like a backward moving agenda process, although not able to induce a single equilibrium outcome, can limit the range of possible outcomes. It has also been seen that these rules are not always successful in defining an equilibrium, such as when two stability-inducing rules are used together, as was shown for the division of the question and a backward moving agenda for sophisticated legislators. This situation also occurs when legislators do not have separable preferences. Furthermore, it has been seen that a number of different assumptions about rules, preferences, and voting strategies can be made and that the resulting number of possible cases increases exponentially.

In this chapter, a different approach to legislative decision making is considered. Rather than examining the stability-inducing effects of specific procedural rules or the effects of various assumptions about preferences, the approach described here seeks to identify a set of very general conditions under which legislative decision making will result in either a unique equilibrium or a relatively small set of possible outcomes.

The Covering Relation

It is assumed in the models discussed below that all collective decisions are made with simple majority voting between pairs of alternatives and that all legislators use sophisticated voting strategies as they were defined in Chapter 3. Further, it is initially assumed that the legislature does not use any restrictive procedural rules such as division of the question.

It might be thought initially that this case looks identical to that in Chapter 4, in which it was seen that in the absence of any restrictive procedural rules, any outcome in the whole issue space was possible. That result, however, assumed that all legislators adopted sincere voting strategies (McKelvey 1976), unlike the present case. For this reason, one interpretation of the analysis here is that it attempts to identify what differences in outcomes can be expected under different assumptions about legislative voting strategies.

In previous chapters, use was made of the concept of a win set, $W(X)$, for some alternative X, defined as the set of alternatives that are majority preferred to X (or that defeat X in majority voting). Following Miller (1977, 1980) who introduced the concept, win sets can be used to define a *covering relation*. Let Y be an element of $W(X)$, so that Y is preferred by a majority to X. Now, as has been seen several times previously, it is often possible to find another alternative Z such that Z is an element of $W(Y)$, and X is an element of $W(Z)$ so that Y defeats X, Z defeats Y, and X defeats Z, producing a social preference cycle. Consider now the case in which Y is an element of $W(X)$, and for any alternative Z that is an element of $W(Y)$, Z is also an element of $W(X)$. No social preference cycle exists in this case because Y defeats X, Z defeats Y, and Z also defeats X. For such cases in which Y defeats X and all Zs that defeat Y also defeat X, Y is said to *cover* X.

An illustration of a covering relation is given in Figure 7.1 for a three-person legislature. It can be seen in this figure that all the alternatives inside two indifference curves through X, constituting $W(X)$, will defeat X because they are majority preferred to X. In this figure, this set is relatively large because X is located relatively far from the geometric center of the three ideal points. Now consider an alternative Y that is an element of $W(X)$. By drawing another set of indifference curves through Y, the win set of Y is defined. This set is shaded in the figure. It can now be seen that all the alternatives in $W(Y)$ are also in the win set of X, so that all alternatives that are majority preferred to Y are also majority preferred to X.

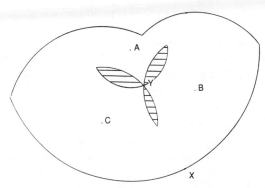

Figure 7.1. Covering Relation for a Three-Person Legislature

As noted above, to say that Y covers X is to imply a lack of a social preference cycle among X, Y, and all the points that defeat Y. This does not imply that social preference cycles may not exist among some alternatives in the issue space. In fact, as seen in Chapter 4, such cycles will be common. What the covering relation does imply, however, is that there is no two-stage social preference cycle among X, Y, and all the points that defeat Y.

It is also straightforward to show that if Y covers X, a majority of sophisticated legislators will never adopt X over Y if Y is one element of the agenda. The fact that Y covers X implies that Y is majority preferred to X and that every alternative that is preferred to Y is also preferred to X. As a consequence, if it can be shown that an alternative is covered by some other alternative on the agenda, the covered alternative can be eliminated from consideration as a possible outcome.

Finally, note in Figure 7.1 that Y is located much closer to the geometric center of the ideal points than is X. This will be seen later to be an important property of covering relations.

Using the preference assumptions listed earlier and the concept of a covering relation, Shepsle and Weingast (1984b) proved several important theorems concerning outcomes when all legislators use sophisticated voting strategies (see also Miller 1980). For such strategies and a given agenda (or order for voting on the alternatives), they defined a *sophisticated agenda equilibrium* as the outcome that will result from the use of the given agenda.[1] They then showed that a fixed length agenda exists with Y as the first alternative and X as the sophisticated agenda equilibrium only if Y does not cover X. Note that what is variable here is the agenda, and what this theorem shows is that with sophisticated voters, it is impossible to construct an agenda starting with Y and leading to the adoption of X if X is covered by Y.

The importance of this result can be seen when it is contrasted with McKelvey's (1976) theorem for sincere voters. McKelvey showed that in the absence of a Plott equilibrium, it was possible to construct a finite agenda from a given starting point which would end with the adoption of any outcome in the whole issue space. This was the basis for the supposed chaos and unpredictability of majority decision making. By this theorem, literally any alternative in the whole issue space was a possible outcome. Shepsle and Weingast's results, however, show that with sophisticated voters, this is no longer the case because if an alternative X is covered by another alternative Y, no agenda from Y to X can be constructed. The starting point of an agenda, in other words, limits the range of possible outcomes.

Suppose now that X is not covered by Y. Shepsle and Weingast also proved that in this case there is an agenda leading from Y to X and that at most, this agenda needs to be only two steps long. Thus, if Y does not cover X, an agenda setter can find an alternative Z such that Z defeats Y, and X defeats Z. Alternatively stated, if Y does not cover X, then there must be an alternative Z such that Z is an element of the win set of Y, and X is an element of the win set of Z.

In general, from the perspective of legislative decision making, there are two basic problems with these results. The first concerns the fact that a forward moving agenda process is being assumed, and as has been noted several times in previous chapters, legislatures generally use a backward moving agenda process. Second, it is being assumed that there is an agenda setter who can dictate which alternatives are considered and in what order. However, as Shepsle and Weingast (1987) noted, this is not true for legislatures like Congress in which any member can propose alternatives to the agenda. The question that needs to be addressed, then, is what implications the above results have in the more realistic case in which a backward moving agenda process and no monopoly agenda setter exist.

Consider first the question of a backward moving agenda process. As noted in the previous chapter, such a process requires that the last vote be between the status quo (or no change in law) and some alternative. What Shepsle and Weingast proved is that with sophisticated voters and a forward moving agenda, an agenda setter can manipulate an agenda so as to start at Y and end with the adoption of X only if Y does not cover X. Given that sophisticated legislators always vote their true preferences on the last vote, the alternative case in which a backward moving agenda process is used implies that alternative X can only be the outcome if it is in the win set of the status quo, $W(Q)$. Moreover, this holds regardless of the location of the starting point or the number of alternatives on the agenda. A backward moving agenda process can thus be seen to be a limit on the power of the agenda setter because in this case, those alternatives that cannot defeat the status quo cannot be outcomes of legislative decision making regardless of the strategies of the agenda setter. This is to be expected, of course, in that a backward moving agenda process is a limit on agenda setting, requiring that the last element in any agenda be the status quo motion.

Consider now the second and more significant issue, which is that agendas in real legislatures like Congress are not controlled by a single agenda setter. Rather, in what is sometimes called an endogenous agenda process, any member of the legislature can propose alternatives so that potentially any alternative in the whole issue space could be on the agenda. Shepsle and Weingast's results do not apply in this more realistic case for the following reason. They have shown that with sophisticated voters, any agenda from Y to X can be reduced to two steps such that the decision process proceeds from Y to Z to X. However, with an endogenous agenda process, any legislator can then extend the agenda by proposing an alternative to X that will defeat X, and except in the special circumstance in which X is the Condorcet winner that defeats all other alternatives, such an alternative will exist. Thus, without an agenda setter with monopoly control of the agenda, no single agenda from Y to X exists.

The more general question, however, is what outcome is to be expected in this more realistic case in which no monopoly agenda setter exists. To examine this question, the concept of an uncovered set is needed.

The Uncovered Set

Consider an alternative W in the issue space X. As seen in the previous section, generally there will be a set of alternatives that W does not cover. Collectively, these alternatives can be called the uncovered set of W or $UC(W)$. Now, consider another alternative, Y, and the set of alternatives not covered by Y, or $UC(Y)$. Proceeding in this way for all alternatives in the issue space, one could define the uncovered set for each alternative. Having done this, one could look at the intersection of all these sets, which would define all the alternatives not covered by any other alternative in the issue space.

This set of alternatives is the uncovered set $UC(X)$ for the whole issue space.

In the Venn diagram representation in Figure 7.2, for example, the uncovered set of Y is represented by one circle and those for W and Z by other circles. For these three alternatives, the uncovered set $UC(X)$ is then the set of alternatives in the shaded area where the three circles intersect because these are the alternatives not covered by any of W, Y, or Z.

Note that as it is defined, the fact that an alternative Y is an element of the uncovered set $UC(X)$ does not imply that Y can defeat all alternatives not in the uncovered set. There can, and generally will, exist alternatives Z not in the uncovered set $UC(X)$ which Y does not cover. From the definition, however, there will be other alternatives in the uncovered set which cover Z. Thus, in Figure 7.2, W covers Z because Z is an element of $UC(W)$. More generally, all alternatives not in the uncovered set must be covered by elements of the set because otherwise these alternatives would be uncovered, and hence would be elements of $UC(X)$.[2] Thus, in general, for any outcome X that is not an element of $UC(X)$, there will be some element of $UC(X)$ which covers Z although a given element of $UC(X)$ may not cover Z.

A very important property of $UC(X)$ is that it always exists (Miller 1980). Moreover, Miller also proved that when a Condorcet alternative exists which defeats all other alternatives, $UC(X)$ consists of just this single alternative. Thus, the minimum size of $UC(X)$ is a

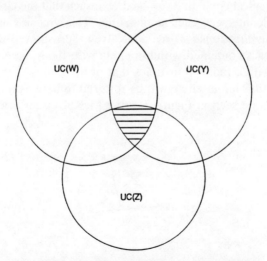

Figure 7.2.   Venn Diagram of the Covering Relation

single alternative. This still leaves open the questions of the maximum size of $UC(X)$, its location in the issue space, and whether or not the expected outcome of legislative decision making will be an element of this set.

Consider first the question of the size of $UC(X)$. In general, the size of $UC(X)$ will depend upon both the distribution of ideal points of the legislators and the nature of the preferences of the legislators (i.e., on the shape of their indifference curves). Moreover, describing the size of $UC(X)$ is complicated by the fact that this set does not necessarily have a simple shape like a circle or ellipse, nor is the shape of $UC(X)$ the same in all cases. In some instances, it is possible for $UC(X)$ to consist of all alternatives, which implies that it is theoretically possible for the size of $UC(X)$ to range from a minimum of one alternative to a maximum of all alternatives. However, if preferences are Euclidean, which implies that the legislators have circular indifference curves, then McKelvey (1986) has shown that the size of the uncovered set can be determined in the following way. For the example in Figure 7.3, first draw median lines through the ideal points of the legislators, where a median line is one in which exactly half of the ideal points are either on the line or to one side. Thus, in Figure 7.3, the line between the ideal points of legislators A and D has two points on the line (those of A and D), one above the line (that of B), and two below the line (those of C and E). Thus, exactly three ideal points are on or above the line, and three are also on the line or below it. Once all the median lines have been drawn, find the smallest circle that can be drawn such that the circumference of this circle intersects each median line.[3] This circle is called the *yolk* or the *generalized median set.* McKelvey then showed that the uncovered set is contained within a circle with the same center as the yolk and with a radius four times that of the radius of the yolk. For reference, this larger circle will be referred to here as the McKelvey set. As can be seen in Figure 7.3, the McKelvey set inscribes a rel-

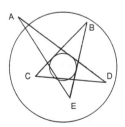

Figure 7.3. McKelvey Set

atively large area. It is important to note that this set is not the uncovered set $UC(X)$, for what McKelvey proved is that $UC(X)$ is contained within the McKelvey set.

McKelvey's limiting of the uncovered set to the McKelvey set is useful in eliminating some alternatives in the issue space. However, as seen in Figure 7.3, this limit can often be quite large. A sometimes more restrictive limit for the Euclidean preference case follows from Miller's (1980) proof that $UC(X)$ is a subset of (or is contained within) $PO(X)$, where $PO(X)$ is the Pareto set.[4] With Euclidean preferences, $PO(X)$ is defined by the set of alternatives inside the lines drawn around the ideal points of the legislators.[5] Thus, in Figure 7.4, repeated from Figure 7.3, the Pareto set consists of all the outcomes within the lines drawn around the five ideal points. By comparing the Pareto set with the McKelvey set (repeated in Figure 7.4), it can be seen that the Pareto set is a more restrictive limit on the size of the uncovered set than is the McKelvey set. Note, however, that this does not imply that the McKelvey set is superfluous, for it can also be seen in Figure 7.4 that in the neighborhood of the ideal point of legislator A, there are alternatives contained in the Pareto set which are not contained in the McKelvey set. Thus, both sets together are sometimes needed to define the maximum limit on the size of $UC(X)$.

As a by-product of these attempts to define the size of the uncovered set, it can also be seen that, at least in the case of Euclidean preferences, this set is usually located near the geometric center of the ideal points of the legislators.[6] This is consistent with Miller's (1980) conjecture that $UC(X)$ is a relatively small set located near the center of the ideal points. It should be noted, however, that if preferences are not Euclidean, it is not presently known what is either the maximum size or location of the uncovered set.

Consider now the question of the relationship of the uncovered set to expected outcomes when legislators use sophisticated voting strategies, and agendas are endogenous. In particular, under these

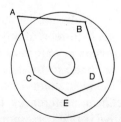

Figure 7.4. McKelvey Set and Pareto Set

assumptions, will the expected outcome be an element of the uncovered set? In general, the answer to this question is both yes and no depending upon the specific details of the way alternative motions are considered. For the kinds of processes typically found in legislatures like Congress, however, the answer to the question is that with sophisticated legislators and an endogenous amendment agenda process, outcomes in the uncovered set are to be expected.

To understand why this is so, consider first a forward moving agenda process and the given alternatives X and Y. If Y covers X, then Y and all the alternatives that defeat Y are preferred to X. From results discussed earlier, with sophisticated legislators, if Y is on the agenda, X cannot be an outcome, for a majority would choose both Y and any alternative that defeats Y rather than choosing X. Moreover, with an endogenous agenda process, any member of the legislature can propose Y, and at least a majority will have an incentive to make such a proposal to eliminate X as a possible outcome.

More generally, what the above argument implies is that every covered alternative can be eliminated as a possible outcome by placing on the agenda an alternative that covers it. If all covered alternatives are eliminated, however, only uncovered ones can be an outcome, implying that the outcome of legislative decision making must be in the uncovered set when legislators adopt sophisticated voting strategies, use an endogenous amendment agenda process, and the agenda is forward moving.

This is a much more general result than the one proved earlier by Shepsle and Weingast. What Shepsle and Weingast showed was that X could not be an outcome if it was covered by Y. This still leaves open the question of whether or not Y can be an outcome—that is, whether or not Y is covered by some other alternative Z on the agenda. In contrast, the result here applies to the whole issue space and implies that any possible outcome must be an element of the uncovered set $UC(X)$. In agenda terms, this means that with sophisticated voting, it is only possible to construct an agenda that terminates in $UC(X)$.

As noted earlier, these results are in sharp contrast to those of McKelvey for sincere voters. Instead of any alternative in the issue space being a potential outcome, outcomes with sophisticated legislators will generally be confined to the uncovered set located near the geometric center of the ideal points of the legislators; and when the legislators have Euclidean preferences, this set will be relatively small. One such alternative is that corresponding to the median preferred outcome on each dimension. Under different assumptions (and most notably, that of separability of preference), this joint median alternative was seen to be a stable equilibrium. In the current example, however, no single alternative is an equilibrium, and what is identified is a range of alternatives as possible outcomes. This range is the uncovered set, and the joint median alternative is an element of this set; another way of characterizing the results here is that the outcome of legislative decision making will be either the joint median alternative or one located relatively near it in the issue space.

The problem with the conclusion that outcomes will be located in the uncovered set, however, is that it is based in part on the assumption of a forward moving agenda process. This is theoretically convenient but empirically incorrect because real legislatures use a backward moving agenda process. The question then is whether or not the result above continues to hold in this more realistic backward moving agenda situation.

As has been seen several times previously, when a backward moving agenda process is used, the only possible outcomes are the status quo Q and $W(Q)$, the win set of the status quo. Assuming that $W(Q)$ is not empty, all the elements of $W(Q)$ are preferred by a majority to Q, so attention here will be focused upon $W(Q)$. This creates two possibilities: one in which $W(Q)$ and the uncovered set $UC(X)$ have elements in common (or where the intersection of $W(Q)$ and $UC(X)$ is not empty), and one in which no common elements exist.

Consider first the case in which $W(Q)$ and $UC(X)$ have common elements. In earlier arguments, it was determined that with an endogenous agenda process, all covered alternatives can be eliminated as possible outcomes. Similarly, with a backward moving agenda, all outcomes not in $W(Q)$ are eliminated. Thus, in this case, the only possible outcomes are those that satisfy both criteria. With a backward moving agenda process, therefore, the only possible outcomes are those that satisfy both criteria, implying that such an agenda process restricts the range of possible outcomes to a subset of the uncovered set.

Now, what if $W(Q)$ and $UC(X)$ do not have any elements in common? Because the backward moving agenda process necessarily restricts outcomes to $W(Q)$, the outcome in this case cannot be in the uncovered set. This is important because it implies that under some legislative rules, outcomes not in the uncovered set are possible (see also Ferejohn, McKelvey, and Packel 1984). However, this does not imply a return to the chaos of McKelvey's theorem because outcomes are still restricted to $W(Q)$ and, à priori, the larger this set, the greater the probability that it will intersect with $UC(X)$.

Congressional Outcomes and the Uncovered Set

Assuming that the intersection of the uncovered set $UC(X)$ and the win set of the status quo $W(Q)$ is not empty, the results above have a number of implications for decision making in legislatures like Congress. One of the most important is that if legislators use sophisticated voting strategies, outcomes will generally be located at not too great a distance from the geometric center of the ideal points of the legislators. Moreover, when legislators have Euclidean preferences, these outcomes will be confined to a relatively small centrally located set. This does not mean that the joint median outcome will be selected, but it does imply that significant deviations from this outcome are not to be expected.

A further set of implications for congressional decision making concerns the relationship between the final outcome and committee recommendations. As noted in Chapter 5, an empirical regularity observed about outcomes in Congress is that committees tend to win when they report their bills to the full chamber. Moreover, winning in this case was seen to involve the fact that few amendments to committee bills are generally approved in the full chamber as well as that those that are approved tend to make only relatively minor changes in committee recommendations. The question that these regularities raise is why such patterns exist.

To answer this question, consider first the possible outcomes in a committee. In doing this, it is assumed that the committee operates with an endogenous backward moving agenda process and that it has gatekeeping powers. From earlier results, this implies that the only possible outcomes in the committee are those in the uncovered set of the committee, which can defeat the status quo motion Q. Call this set the feasible set for the committee or FS_C, and note that in formal terms, $FS_C = \{X | X \in W_C(Q) \cap UC_C(X)\}$, where the C subscript denotes the committee. In an analogous fashion, the full chamber will only adopt an alternative that is in the uncovered set of the full chamber and that can also defeat Q. Call this set the feasible set for the full chamber or FS_F. In formal terms, $FS_F = \{X | X \in W_F(Q) \cap UC_F(X)\}$ where the F subscript denotes the full chamber. The question then is when will a committee of sophisticated legislators report a bill to their full chamber.

Note first that no bill will be reported if the intersection of $W_C(Q)$ and $W_F(Q)$ is empty because this implies that there is no bill preferred by both committee and full chamber majorities to the status quo. Also note that the committee will only report a bill that is an element of FS_C, and the full chamber will only pass a bill that is an element of FS_F. However, these are only initial conditions, because a sophisticated committee majority will only report a bill if they can be sure that the full chamber will not amend it in such a way that this committee majority would rather have the extant status quo remain in effect. This implies that the committee will only report a bill if FS_F is contained in FS_C—that is, if the set of feasible bills that the full chamber can pass is contained in the set of feasible bills that the committee can report. Stated another way, this says that committees will only report bills that a committee majority anticipates will not be altered in any major way by the full chamber.

Thus, the question of why congressional committees are apparently so successful in having their recommendations accepted has a relatively simple answer: they only report bills when FS_F is contained in FS_C and when neither of these sets is empty. Further, by only reporting bills that meet these requirements, no amendments that move the outcome outside of this set will be successful, assuming a relatively small uncovered set in the full chamber, this implies that only relatively small adjustments to committee bills will be made in the full chamber. Thus, from this perspective, committees may appear to have proposal power simply because they are using a sophisticated strategy of confining themselves to reporting only bills that meet the requirements above.

Summary and Conclusions

It has been seen in this chapter that under a set of fairly general assumptions, legislative decision making by sophisticated legislators will result in outcomes from a relatively small set located near the geometric center of the ideal points of the legislature. Moreover, it was seen that this conclusion holds for both the endogenous amendment and backward moving agenda processes typically found in legislatures like the U.S. Congress. Finally, it has been seen that the empirical regularities of committee success in Congress can be accounted for by the uncovered set analysis above. The question still remains, however, of whether or not this is an adequate and appropriate explanation for the outcomes of decision-making processes of real legislatures.

There are two possible problems with the foregoing analysis as an empirically valid explanation. One concerns the various rules that real legislatures like Congress use in making collective decisions, and the second concerns the assumption that all legislators adopt sophisticated voting strategies.

Consider first the question of how various rules of procedure can affect whether or not outcomes in the uncovered set will occur. As noted earlier, it is currently not known whether or not the results implying outcomes in the uncovered set hold for all the procedural rules used in real legislatures. One case in which an uncovered set outcome is not expected is when a backward moving agenda process is used, and the win set of the status quo does not intersect with the uncovered set. It is not currently known whether this is a special exception or is indicative of more general problems with the uncovered set as a source of outcomes of legislative decision making. As McKelvey (1986) has noted, the relationship between institutional arrangements and the expectation of outcomes in the uncovered set needs considerably more research.

A second difficulty with using these theoretical results as an explanation of decision making in real legislatures is the assumption that all legislators adopt sophisticated voting strategies. Developing such strategies requires knowledge of the ideal points of all other legislators and an ability to calculate expected outcomes based upon this knowledge. Both of these requirements would appear to be unrealistic for real legislators, especially those in relatively large legislatures like the 100-member Senate and 435-member House. On the other hand, an argument could be made that through the long experience of members (and many members of Congress have long careers) and the information-gathering system that both parties maintain in their whip systems, the prerequisites for developing sophisticated strategies do exist. The existence of prerequisites, however, is not the same thing as the actual development and use of such strategies by real legislators. Because it is currently not known whether or not real legislators actually develop and use sophisticated voting strategies, the extent to which the theoretical results concerning the uncovered set can explain outcomes in real legislatures is also unclear.

The comments above indicate that theoretical models based upon sophisticated voting may or may not be able to explain empirical regularities in real legislatures. This is only half the story. What is also important is that at a theoretical level, the results suggest that legislative decision making need not be as chaotic and unpredictable as thought previously. This is important because it implies that, at least in principle, legislative decision making can work as was intended in democratic theory.

CONCLUSION

∎ ∎ ∎ ∎ ∎

The examination of the logic of lawmaking through the spatial theory of legislatures in previous chapters has focused primarily on the extent to which it can explain empirical regularities in legislatures like Congress. It has been seen that the theory has had some success in explaining these regularities as well as in providing an integrated framework for understanding more generally how legislative processes work. It should be noted, however, that from the perspective of legislative scholars, the regularities for which the theory can presently account are relatively large scale. Many other more specific regularities that have been identified in the empirical literature on legislative decision making are not addressed at all. Thus, the theory can account for the general success of committees in having their recommendations adopted in their full chambers but does not address the question of why there are systematic differences in the success rates of different committees. Similarly, the theory can account for the effects on outcomes that some rules like division of the question or a backward moving agenda have, but the hundreds of other rules typically found in real legislatures are ignored.

The basic reason that spatial theory has had only some success in accounting for some of the macro-level regularities in real legislatures is that the type of legislative decision making assumed in the theory has been relatively simple and stylized and ignores most of the richness and complexity of that found in real legislatures. As a first step in theory development, this is understandable because all scientific theories are simplifications of the phenomena with which they are concerned; this is especially true in the early stages of theory development. However, once the underlying fundamentals have been established, greater correspondence between the assumptions and hypotheses of the theory and empirical reality needs to develop. As Panning (1985, 686) has noted, "representations that are known to be too simple or even counterfactual can be useful nonetheless, for they may provide important clues to the development of more adequate representations." In terms of the spatial theory of legislatures, the recent incorporation into the theory of various forms of procedural rules typically found in real legislatures has begun this process, so there appears to be an increasing degree of harmony between the assumptions underlying the theory and the kinds of decision-making processes found in legislatures like Congress. In addition, students of legislatures have recently begun to subject the theory to rigorous empirical testing, abandoning the simple argument-by-analogy style of establishing correlation between theoretical and empirical propositions. Considerably more of this needs to be done, but the progress that has been made over the past decade is encouraging.

It should also be noted, however, that holding the spatial theory to a high standard of empirical validity may not always be perceived as appropriate because it is not often clear what the purpose of the theory is. As a result, it is unclear just what kind of theory is being developed and by what criteria it should be judged. One possibility is that spatial theory is purely axiomatic or mathematical and is intended to establish logical relationships among a set of abstract mathematical concepts. In this interpretation, the significance of the theory is to be judged by the nature of the theorems it allows to be proved and by whether or not these are mathematically elegant, significant, and interesting. Viewed in this light, the theory is not necessarily intended to imply anything about real-world decision making, and therefore questioning the empirical validity of the theory is inappropriate.

Alternatively, it could be argued that the spatial theory is intended to be part of normative democratic theory. This is the interpretation stressed by Plott (1976) in his extensive review of theory development through the mid-1970s. Plott notes that normative criteria and justifications have been present from the beginning of modern social choice theory. Black (1948) and Arrow (1951), for example, explicitly built normative criteria into their models of collective choice. Viewed as a part of normative democratic theory, the primary purpose of spatial theory is to examine and explain how democratic decision making works in its pure or ideal form, not how it operates in practice in legislatures. Specifically, the purpose of the theory in this interpretation is to answer the question of what conditions are necessary and/or sufficient for a pure democratic decision-making process to produce a socially optimal decision. In this case, as in the mathematical theory case above, the criterion for judging the theory is not empirical validity but rather the extent to which it can provide insightful answers to the perennial questions of democratic theory.

Finally, spatial theory could be interpreted as an empirical theory designed to explain the regularities of decision making in real-world situations. This is the interpretation that has been stressed here as well as by Panning (1983, 1985), Shepsle (1985), and Krehbiel (1988). Moreover, a strong argument can be made for why, ultimately, this must be the primary purpose of formal models in general and the spatial theory of legislatures in particular. One part of this argument is that this is what the theorists frequently claim they are doing. McKelvey (1986, 283–84), for example, argues that "there appears to be enough commonality among the outcomes selected under different institutional arrangements so that non-trivial bounds on social choice, which hold under several different institutions, can be determined." This is clearly using empirical criteria as a guide for theoretical development, and the implication is that the theory developed will be capable of explaining empirical regularities. In addition, it has been the inconsistency between theoretical results and empirical observation that has primarily stimulated theory development over the past decade. This is most clearly seen in the efforts reviewed in Chapters 5, 6, and 7 to answer Tullock's question of "Why so much stability?" in real-world decision making. If the primary purpose of spatial theory was not to be empirically valid, this question would not have been significant.

A second part of the argument concerns the relative importance of mathematical, normative, and empirical theories generally. Although interesting in their own right, ultimately, both mathematical and normative theories are tools for helping us to understand better the world in which we live. Thus, it may be interesting to know that a certain way of setting up a democratic decision-making process is optimal in the sense of maximizing the correspondence between individual values and social choices. However, the importance of such a result is lessened if it is empirically impossible to establish such a system in the real world. It would be of considerably more interest and importance if the empirical consequences of an empirically feasible decision-making structure could be assessed.

Accepting the arguments above, some directions that spatial theory development needs to take in the future can be identified. One of these is to incorporate more realistic underlying assumptions into the theory. In its present form, the theory is largely a deterministic one, which implies that the way a given legislative decision maker may act in a given situation always has a probability of zero or one. According to the theory, each legislator knows in every situation exactly what action is the most appropriate for maximizing his or her utility and then takes this action. The smallest difference in utility between two alternatives is ignored; a legislator will always vote for the most preferred alternative even when the difference between two alternatives is vanishingly small. However, our own experiences suggest that this is not correct, and the empirical evidence from all the social sciences supports this conclusion. People are not deterministic actors. As a result, it seems clear that in the future, the deterministic component of spatial theory needs to be replaced with a stochastic one that makes the behavior of legislators probabilistic. Moreover, as work by Ferejohn, McKelvey, and Packel (1984) and by Feld, Grofman, and Miller (1985) suggests, the incorporation of such a component into extant theory can be done in a relatively straightforward way that does not require a major theoretical overhaul.[1]

A second area in which theory development is needed concerns the costs of decision making. In its current form, spatial theory assumes that such costs do not exist (or are not considered by legislative actors). In the sophisticated voting version of the theory, for example, legislators are assumed to know with certainty the preferences of all the other members of the legislature. Moreover, once they have this information, it is assumed that they can calculate their own sophisticated voting strategies. However, empirically, acquiring and processing information is a costly undertaking, and once this is recognized, there is the possibility that legislators might not always be willing to bear some or all of these costs. In turn, this will affect their voting behavior in the legislature. However, until information and decision costs are systematically incorporated into spatial theory, it is unclear exactly what changes in behavior will occur and what the consequences are for legislative outcomes.

A third area of theory development concerns legislative rules and procedures. As noted earlier, over the past decade, a significant amount of progress has been made in incorporating into the theory procedures found in real legislatures. More of this needs to be done, however, before the theory can explain empirical outcomes in procedurally complex legislatures. Even more significantly, as seen in Chapter 6, the way in which various rules and procedures interact with each other needs to be examined.

Finally, a much more sophisticated and rigorous program of empirically testing the theory must be established. This is especially important for theorists as they begin to incorporate more realistic assumptions and procedures into spatial theory. In any given instance, there are always many possible ways that such things can be built into the theory, and it is unclear which way is empirically the most appropriate. Testing theoretical hypotheses against empirical cases does not always provide the correct answer to this problem, but it does tend to reduce the number of options and thereby facilitates the development of empirically valid theory.

Undertaking all the tasks noted above is a very big job, and doing them all will take time. However, progress in all these areas is steadily being made, and, as a result, it appears that spatial theory offers a very good prospect of being the first rigorous and systematic empirical theory of legislative decision making.

NOTES

■　■　■　■　■

Introduction

1. *Congressional Quarterly Almanac, 1985* (Washington, D.C., Congressional Quarterly, 1986), 286.

2. An excellent example of this form of explanation is Birnbaum and Murray's (1987) analysis of the 1986 Tax Reform Act.

3. A major exception is Fenno's (1966) study of the House and Senate Appropriations Committees in which he presents a detailed analysis of why various funding provisions get included in, or excluded from, appropriations bills.

Chapter 1
Definitions and Assumptions

1. For a general discussion of rational actor theories, see Buchanan and Tullock (1962) or Riker and Ordeshook (1973). For a discussion of such theories in political science, see Panning (1985).

2. One example is the literature on roll-call voting in Congress in which it has been found consistently that the best single predictor of how a member will vote is his or her party (Kingdon, 1973).

3. For a detailed statement of cue-taking behavior in Congress, see Matthews and Stimpson (1970).

4. For a full statement of these arguments, see Simon (1957) or Lindblom (1965).

5. See, for example, Tversky and Kahneman (1982).

6. It might be thought that an additional relationship of "I don't know which I prefer" could exist among these alternatives. However, this relationship is equivalent to preferring them equally because if one does not know which alternative he or she prefers, it is impossible for one alternative to be ranked before another, and hence they must be ranked equally.

7. von Neumann and Morgenstern (1947) have shown how, through the use

of a lottery over the alternatives, cardinal (or interval level) utility can be measured (see also Riker and Ordeshook 1973). However, their proposal is theoretically controversial; practically, for the case of real-world legislatures, implementing such a procedure would be impossible. Therefore, here, as in the spatial theory generally, only ordinal utility will be assumed.

8. An additional consequence is that one cannot add the utilities of different actors to get an aggregate level of satisfaction from a given outcome.

9. More generally, where R represents "preferred to or indifferent to," transitive preferences imply that BRA and ARQ implies BRQ.

10. In making this assumption, it is not denied that people may at times hold intransitive preferences. However, because people cannot act rationally on the basis of such preferences, they cannot logically be a part of a theory of rational action.

11. Note in the figure that there are just three preference curves, one for each of the groups. This is permissible here as the groups are of equal size. Normally, however, one would draw a separate indifference curve for each legislator. Thus, in Figure 1.3, one would draw 435 separate indifference curves.

12. Technically, the single-peak condition is sufficient for the existence of a majority-preferred outcome. It is not, however, a necessary condition. The (technical) necessary conditions are given in Sen and Pattanaik (1969).

13. Technically, the equilibrium noted in the text is attractive and stable. It is attractive in the sense that it is the alternative toward which the outcome will move, and it is stable in the sense that once this alternative is reached, it will not be departed from. As shown later, however, not all voting equilibria need be attractive. For a detailed analysis of the meaning of a spatial equilibrium, see Krehbiel (1988).

14. Condorcet voting is named after the Marquis de Condorcet (1743–94), a French mathematician, philosopher, and social scientist who was the first to examine such a voting scheme systematically. For an analysis of Condorcet's work, see Black (1958). The specific method described here differs from pure Condorcet voting in that all logical combinations are not paired against each other. Here, only winners make it to the next round.

15. Alternative voting schemes are discussed in Riker and Ordeshook (1973), Riker (1982), and Ordeshook (1986).

16. One other condition is needed here, and that is that all the voters vote their true preferences. As will be seen subsequently, there are reasons that actors might not do this in a legislature.

Chapter 2
The Unidimensional Model of Legislative Decision Making

1. What is not known are the second most preferred positions for members in the middle, so it is unclear, for example, whether the preference curve for the member who most prefers the $2000 increase should decline faster on the left or right of the $2000 point. However, in this case (and in many similar cases), this issue is not a problem and does not affect the conclusions reached.

2. CM, in other words, is the outcome corresponding to the median preference

curve peak when only the preferences of committee members are considered. Similarly, *FM* is the median peak at which the preferences of all the members of a chamber are considered.

3. Under congressional rules in which the full chamber does not consider bills until they have been reported by a committee, it might seem here that the optimal strategy for the committee might be to report no bill, ensuring themselves the status quo outcome. However, such a strategy presumes that a committee majority will adopt a sophisticated strategy, and such strategies will not be considered until the next chapter. Thus, here, it is assumed that the committee majority is myopic and reports the *CM* bill.

4. See also Niemi (1983) for the effects of partially relaxing the single peakedness requirement.

5. Arrow's conditions are somewhat technical and will not be discussed here. For a discussion and analysis of them, see Plott (1976).

6. Note that the existence of a social preference cycle does not always imply that an equilibrium does not exist. There may exist, for example, an alternative that defeats all others even when there are cycles among these latter alternatives.

7. *ST* is preferred to *IT* by groups 2, 3, 4, and 5, which have a total of 194 members. *IT* is preferred to *ST* only by group 1, with 162 members. Thus, $ST > IT$. Similarly, *IT* is preferred to *ET* by groups 1 and 3, with a total of 178 members; *ET* is preferred by groups 2 and 4, with 107 members; and it is unclear which order is preferred by group 5. However, if only one member of group 5 prefers *IT* to *ET*, there would be 179 members preferring *IT* to *ET* and only 177 members preferring *ET* to *IT*. Thus, it is reasonable to presume that $IT > ET$. Finally, groups 1 and 2, with 200 members, prefer *ET* to *ST*, whereas groups 3, 4, and 5, with 156 members, prefer *ST* to *ET*. Thus, $ET > ST$, and the whole social preference order is intransitive.

Chapter 3
Sincere and Sophisticated Voting

1. It is important to note here that Black's result holds when *all* voters behave sincerely and, as will be shown subsequently, when *all* use sophisticated strategies. Black's result does not hold when *some* voters use sincere while others use sophisticated strategies.

2. Farquharson (1969) proved that with a binary agenda (where all decisons are between two alternatives) and with actors not indifferent between any two alternatives, sophisticated voting leads to a determinant outcome even when preference orders cannot be represented by single-peaked curves.

3. Sophistication on the part of a committee majority has no impact on this conclusion because a floor majority prefers Q to any position to the right of Q, whereas a committee majority prefers Q to any point to the left of Q. Thus, there is no point preferred by both majorities to Q, and Q will win.

4. Note that in the earlier example, the saving amendment was the Condorcet winner, and this was possible without the revised definition. With the revised definition, this is no longer possible.

5. For additional cases, see Enelow and Koehler (1980).

6. *Congressional Quarterly Almanac, 1966*, 460; quoted in Enelow (1981, 1073).

7. Another possible reason that some representatives did not adopt sophisticated strategies is the electoral constraint they faced. Representatives from liberal districts where the bill with the Powell amendment was strongly preferred may have judged that they would have difficulty explaining to their constituents why they adopted a sophisticated strategy and voted against the amendment. For these legislators, the electorally safe strategy was to vote for the amendment and hope it would not kill the whole bill.

Chapter 4
Multidimensional Decision-Making Models

1. The distance between *IP* and *A* is given by the square root of $(5000 - 4500)^2 + (6000 - 3216)^2$, which equals 2828, and that between *IP* and *CP* is given by the square root of $(5000 - 3000)^2 + (6000 - 4000)^2$, which is again equal to 2828.

2. More technically, if $u(X) > u(Y)$ and $u(Z) = a(u(X)) + (1 - a)u(Y)$, then $u(Z) > u(Y)$ when $0 < a < 1$.

3. In the literature on multiple dimension models, it is unclear how an actor will vote if he or she is indifferent between two outcomes. Such an actor may abstain or may choose randomly (e.g., by flipping a coin). Consistent with the literature, this question will not be addressed here, and it will be assumed that such a possibility is unlikely to arise.

4. This is possible because with separable preferences, the legislators' preferences in each dimension are not affected by positions on the other dimension, and hence they would not reorder their preferences if the other dimension did not exist.

5. Note here that it makes no difference whether the ideal points are listed from top down or bottom up. *C* is the median ideal point in either case.

6. For a more detailed analysis of this result as well as an insightful intuitive geometric presentation, see Feld and Grofman (1987).

7. See, for example, Halfpenny and Taylor (1973), Plott and Levine (1978), and Krehbiel (1985).

8. According to Schelling, decision makers will generally select some obvious or prominent point as the group decision. In a 100 by 100 space, for example, the (50, 50) point in the middle might be thought of as an obvious point. In their experiments, Fiorina and Plott took as the obvious point the ideal point that was located in the middle of the other ideal points.

9. In interpreting his results, Wilson also showed that his subjects consistently adopted sincere (or myopic) rather than sophisticated voting strategies.

Chapter 5
The Return to Equilibrium: Controlling Legislative Agendas

1. An alternative way for legislator A to proceed if he or she has complete agenda control is to prevent outcome *Z* from being considered. This could be accomplished by scheduling a single vote between *X* and *Y*.

2. It is assumed here that it is not possible to add alternatives to the agenda. Were it so, it would generally be possible to find and propose an alternative that would defeat Y. For a consideration of this issue, see Riker (1980).

3. The House also uses a backward moving agenda process that requires that the last vote be between the surviving alternative and the status quo. Such a rule, however, is not imposed here.

4. This assumes a forward moving agenda process. The alternative of a backward moving agenda process is considered in the next chapter.

5. In win set terms, Q is an element of the win set of every alternative to its left.

6. Note that rearranging the alternatives in Figure 5.3 will not allow for all the preference curves to be single peaked. One way this can be seen is by noting that of the labeled positions, X defeats M, M defeats Y, and Y defeats X, so that the social preferences are necessarily intransitive regardless of the ordering of the alternatives.

7. It is assumed that all legislators adopt sincere voting strategies and also that a forward moving agenda process is used. As is shown in the next two chapters, these are both crucial assumptions because if either of them is dropped, the power of an agenda setter to manipulate outcomes is significantly reduced.

8. As in all cases involving Congress, there can be exceptions to the statement that all bills are immediately referred to a standing committee. One kind of exception would be the referral of a bill to a committee specifically constituted to deal with it. As a general rule, however, the statement is accurate for almost all bills introduced.

9. These figures are taken from the Daily Digest "Resume of Congressional Activities" in the *Congressional Record*.

10. The discharging of committees is covered in Rule 27 in the House and Rule 17 in the Senate. In both cases, a discharge requires the support of a majority of the membership.

11. In the 99th Congress (1985–86), for example, House committees reported 574 House bills, of which 503 were passed in the full House, a success rate of 87.6 percent.

12. Fleisher and Bond (1981), using only amendments that were accepted or rejected on a roll-call vote during the 94th Congress (1975–76), found that 35 percent of proposed amendments were adopted in the House and 37 percent in the Senate.

13. Similarly, Bach (1980) reported that during the period from 1973 to 1978, fourteen closed rules were reported in the House, and twelve of them were considered by the full chamber. Of these twelve, only one was rejected.

14. In the 99th Congress, there were eighteen modified open rules and seventeen modified closed rules. In contrast, there were sixty-five open rules.

15. Committees also frequently claim that they are representative of the full chamber and have attempted to put together a package consistent with the will of the full chamber (or a chamber majority).

Chapter 6
The Return to Equilibrium: Controlling Legislative Agendas

1. Experimentally, however, as Wilson (1986) has shown, the status quo does appear to be advantaged. In his backward moving agenda experiments, the status quo position was the outcome in two out of three cases.

2. Note that in considering the impact of a division of the question rule on legislative decision making, it will not initially be assumed that a backward moving agenda process is operating. This allows for the impact of a division of the question to be considered independently of other rules.

3. D is the median here because on dimension 1, there are two ideal points to the left of D (those of A and C) and two to the right (those of B and E).

4. It could also be shown that the starting point of the decision-making process does not affect the eventual outcome.

5. Ordeshook actually considered four possibilities. In addition to the rules discussed here, he considered one similar to that used by Shepsle (1979), which is considered later in this chapter. He also considered one that allows an agenda with a prespecified order of voting on the issues.

6. See also Shepsle and Weingast (1981).

7. Consideration of this last question should logically precede consideration of the other two. However, here, because of the complexity involved in addressing it and the number of different cases that can arise, it will be considered last.

8. It is straightforward to show that this conclusion also holds when repeated consideration of the dimensions is allowed.

9. Such majorities must exist because as defined here, Q cannot be a Plott equilibrium, which, when it exists, is equivalent to the median in each dimension. Similarly, the fact that assumption Q defeats X implies that X is also not a Plott equilibrium.

10. As Bach (1987) noted, Congress operates on the principle that a rule is not in effect until it is invoked by a member. Thus, the simple fact that a division of the question rule exists is not sufficient to conclude that congressional policy making proceeds according to it. This conclusion is only valid if members self-impose the rule on themselves and do not offer motions that contain several dimensions or if the rule is invoked when multidimensional motions are made.

11. This is because at the position Y_1, the indifference curve closest to his or her ideal point is tangent to (or just touches) the vertical line drawn through X_1. This implies that, given the fixed X_1 position, Y_1 is the point closest to this legislator's ideal point, giving him or her the maximum possible utility.

12. In this example, it is assumed that the legislators continue to consider a given dimension until they have reached an equilibrium position, and no other movements are possible. An alternative way of proceeding would be for them to switch dimensions as soon as a motion defeating the previous status quo motion on that dimension was adopted. Denzau and Mackay (1981) have shown, however, that such an alteration in procedure would not alter the conclusion about reaching an equilibrium in the present case as long as repeated consideration of the dimensions were allowed.

13. For a similar case, see Black and Newing (1951).

Chapter 7
The Return to Equilibrium: Sophisticated Voting and Uncovered Sets

1. See Shepsle and Weingast (1984b) for more precise and formal definitions.

2. As it is defined, the uncovered set is similar to the V-set of von Neumann and Morgenstern (1944). For n-person games, the V-set consists of outcomes that satisfy the properties of internal stability (i.e., no element of the set dominates, or is better, than any other element of the set) and external stability (i.e., for any outcome not in the set, there is an element of the set that dominates it). McKelvey (1986) has shown that V-set solutions are contained in the uncovered set.

3. A circle is the appropriate term here for the two-dimensional case in Figure 7.3. In the more general case of an n-dimensional issue space, the circle would be a ball.

4. The definition of the Pareto set in words is somewhat complicated. In general, an alternative X is an element of this set if there does not exist another alternative that all actors like at least as much as X and that at least one actor prefers to X. Alternatively, consider two alternatives, X and Y. If at least one actor prefers X to Y, and all other actors either prefer X to Y or are indifferent between X and Y, then a move from Y to X is a Pareto move. The Pareto set can then be defined as the set of alternatives for which no Pareto moves are possible.

5. This geometric set is sometimes called the *convex hull* of the ideal points.

6. There are some exceptions to this for certain set of preferences but generally $UC(X)$ is at or near the center.

Conclusion

1. In addition to making spatial theory more empirically realistic, the works cited in the text also suggest that replacement of a deterministic component with a stochastic one can lead to the identification of additional cases in which legislative decision making has a stable equilibrium.

REFERENCES

■　■　■　■

Arrow, Kenneth J. 1951. *Social choice and individual value*. New Haven: Yale University Press.

Bach, Stanley. 1980. The structure of choice in the House of Representatives: Recent uses of special rules. Paper presented at the 1980 Annual Meeting of the American Political Science Association, Washington, D.C.

———. 1984. Resolving legislative differences in Congress: An introduction to conference committees and amendments between the chambers. Congressional Reference Service. Unpublished manuscript.

———. 1987. The nature of congressional rules. Paper presented at the 1987 Annual Meeting of the American Political Science Association, Chicago.

Birnbaum, Jeffrey H., and Alan S. Murray. 1987. *Showdown at Gucci gulch*. New York: Vintage.

Black, Duncan. 1948. On the rationale of group decision making. *Journal of Political Economy* 56:22–34.

———. 1958. *The theory of committees and elections*. Cambridge: Cambridge University Press.

Black, Duncan, and R. A. Newing. 1951. *Committee decisions with complementary valuation*. London: William Hodge.

Blydenburgh, John. 1971. The closed rule and the paradox of voting. *Journal of Politics* 33:57–71.

Braybrook, David, and Charles E. Lindblom. 1962. *A strategy of decision*. New York: Free Press.

Buchanan, James M., and Gordon Tullock. 1962. *The Calculus of Consent*. Ann Arbor: University of Michigan Press.

DeMayer, Frank, and Charles Plott. 1970. The probability of a cyclical majority. *Econometrica* 38:345–54.

Denzau, Arthur T., and Robert J. Mackay. 1980. Benefit and tax share discrimination by a monopoly bureau. *Journal of Public Economics* 13:341–68.

———. 1981. Structure-induced equilibria and perfect-foresight expectations. *American Journal of Political Science* 25:762–79.

―――. 1983. Gatekeeping and monopoly power of committees: An analysis of sincere and sophisticated behavior. *American Journal of Political Science* 27:740–61.

Enelow, James M. 1981. Saving amendments, killer amendments, and an expected utility theory of sophisticated voting. *Journal of Politics* 28:587–97.

Enelow, James M., and David H. Koehler. 1980. The amendment in legislative strategy: Sophisticated voting in the U.S. Congress. *Journal of Politics* 42:396–413.

Farquharson, Robin. 1969. *Theory of voting.* New Haven: Yale University Press.

Feld, Scott L., and Bernard Grofman. 1987. Majority rule outcomes and the structure of debate in one-issue-at-a-time decision making. State University of New York at Stony Brook. Unpublished manuscript.

Feld, Scott L., Bernard Grofman, and Nicholas R. Miller. 1985. Cycle lengths, the uncovered set, and other features of majority preferences in the spatial context. Paper presented at the Weingast Conference of Models of Voting, California Institute of Technology.

Fenno, Richard F. 1966. *The power of the purse: Appropriations politics in Congress.* Boston: Little, Brown.

―――. 1973. *Congressmen in committees.* Boston: Little, Brown.

Ferejohn, John M., Richard D. McKelvey, and Edward W. Packel. 1984. Limiting distributions for continuous state Markov models. *Social Choice and Welfare* 1:45–68.

Fiorina, Morris P., and Charles Plott. 1978. Committee decisions under majority rule: An experimental study. *American Political Science Review* 72:575–98.

Fleisher, Richard, and Jon R. Bond. 1981. Beyond committee control: An empirical analysis of the success of floor amendments in the U.S. Congress. Paper presented at the 39th Annual Meeting of the Midwest Political Science Association, Cincinnati, Ohio.

Gehrlein, William V., and Peter C. Fishburn. 1976. The probability of the paradox of voting. *Journal of Economic Theory* 13:14–25.

Halfpenny, Peter, and Michael Taylor. 1973. An experimental study of individual and collective decision making. *British Journal of Political Science* 3:425–44.

Jillson, Calvin C., and Rick K. Wilson. 1987. A social choice model of politics: Insights into the demise of the U.S. Continental Congress. *Legislative Studies Quarterly* 12:5–32.

Kadane, Joseph B. 1972. On division of the question. *Public Choice* 13:47–54.

Kingdon, John W. 1973. *Congressmen's voting decisions.* New York: Harper and Row.

Kramer, Gerald H. 1972. Sophisticated voting over multidimensional choice spaces. *Journal of Mathematical Sociology* 2:165–81.

Krehbiel, Keith. 1985. Obstruction and representation in legislatures. *American Journal of Political Science* 29:643–59.

―――. 1987. Sophisticated committees and structure-induced equilibria in Congress. In *Congress: Structure and policy,* ed. Matthew McCubbins and Terry Sullivan. Cambridge: Cambridge University Press.

―――. 1988. Spatial models of legislative choice. *Legislative Studies Quarterly* 13:259–319.

Lindblom, Charles. 1965. *The intelligence of democracy*. New York: Free Press.

Mackay, Robert J., and Carolyn L. Weaver. 1978. Monopoly bureaus and fiscal outcomes. In *Policy analysis and deductive reasoning*, ed. G. Tullock and R. Wagner. Lexington, Mass.: Heath.

————. 1981. Agenda control by budget maximizers in a multi-bureau setting. *Public Choice* 37:481–91.

————. 1983. Commodity bundling and agenda control in the public sector. *Quarterly Journal of Economics* 98:611–35.

Manley, John. 1970. *The politics of finance*. Boston: Little, Brown.

Matthews, Donald R., and James A. Stimpson, 1970. Decision-making by U.S. representatives. In *Political decision-making*, ed. S. Sidney Ulmer. New York: Van Nostrand.

McKelvey, Richard D. 1976. Intransitivities in multidimensional voting models and some implications for agenda control. *Journal of Economic Theory* 12:472–82.

————. 1979. General conditions for global intransitivities in formal voting models. *Econometrica* 47:1085–111.

————. 1986. Covering, dominance, and institution free properties of social choice. *American Journal of Political Science* 30:283–314.

McKelvey, Richard D., and Richard G. Niemi. 1978. A multistage game representation of sophisticated voting for binary procedures. *Journal of Economic Theory* 18:1–22.

Miller, Nicholas R. 1977. Graph-theoretical approaches to the theory of voting. *American Journal of Political Science* 21:769–803.

————. 1980. A new solution set for tournaments and majority voting. *American Journal of Political Science* 24:68–96.

Niemi, Richard G. 1983. Why so much stability: Another opinion. *Public Choice* 41:261–70.

Niemi, Richard G., and Herbert Weisberg. 1968. A mathematical solution for the probability of the paradox of voting. *Behavioral Science* 13:317–23.

Ordeshook, Peter C. 1986. *Game theory and political theory*. Cambridge: Cambridge University Press.

Panning, William H. 1983. Formal models of legislative processes. *Legislative Studies Quarterly* 7:427–55.

————. 1985. Formal models of legislative processes. In *Handbook of Legislative Research*, ed. Gerhard Loewenberg, Samuel C. Patterson, and Malcolm E. Jewell. Cambridge: Harvard University Press.

Plott, Charles R. 1967. A notion of equilibrium and its possibility under majority rule. *American Economic Review* 57:787–806.

————. 1976. Axiomatic social choice theory: An interpretation and overview. *American Journal of Political Science* 20:511–56.

Plott, Charles, and Michael Levine. 1978. A model of agenda control influence on committee decisions. *American Economic Review* 68:146–60.

Rae, Douglas, and Michael Taylor. 1971. Decision rules and policy outcomes. *British Journal of Political Science* 1:71–90.

Riker, William H. 1958. The paradox of voting and congressional rules for voting amendments. *American Political Science Review* 52:349–66.

————. 1965. Arrow's theorem and some examples of the paradox of voting. In

Mathematical Applications in Political Science, ed. John Claunch. Dallas: Southern Methodist University Press.

———. 1980. Implications from the disequilibrium of majority rule for the study of institutions. *American Political Science Review* 74:432–46.

———. 1982. *Liberalism against populism*. San Francisco: W. H. Freeman.

Riker, William H., and Peter C. Ordeshook. 1973. *An introduction to positive political theory*. Englewood Cliffs: Prentice-Hall.

Romer, Thomas, and Howard Rosenthal. 1978. Political resource allocation, controlled agendas, and the status quo. *Public Choice* 33:27–43.

Schelling, Thomas C. 1960. *The strategy of conflict*. Oxford: Oxford University Press.

Schofield, Norman J. 1978. Instability of simple dynamic games. *The Review of Economic Studies* 45:575–94.

Sen, A. K., and P. K. Pattanaik. 1969. Necessary and sufficient conditions for rational choice under majority decision. *Journal of Economic Theory* 1:178–202.

Shepsle, Kenneth A. 1979. Institutional arrangements and equilibrium in multidimensional voting models. *American Journal of Political Science* 23:27–59.

———. 1985. Prospects for formal models of legislatures. *Legislative Studies Quarterly* 10:5–19.

Shepsle, Kenneth A., and Barry R. Weingast. 1981. Structure-induced equilibrium and legislative choice. *Public Choice* 37:503–15.

———. 1984a. When do rules of procedure matter? *Journal of Politics* 46:206–21.

———. 1984b. Uncovered sets and sophisticated voting outcomes with implications for agenda institutions. *American Journal of Political Science* 81:85–104.

———. 1987. The institutional foundations of committee power. *American Political Science Review* 81:85–127.

Simon, Herbert. 1957. *Models of Man*. New York: John Wiley.

Smith, Steven. 1987. Sequence, position, goals, and committee power. The Brookings Institution, Washington, D.C. Unpublished manuscript.

Tullock, Gordon. 1981. Why so much stability? *Public Choice* 37:189–202.

Tversky, Amos, and Daniel Kahneman. 1982. *Judgement under uncertainty: Heuristics and biases*. Cambridge: Cambridge University Press.

von Neumann, John, and Oskar Morgenstern. 1944. *The theory of games and economic behavior*. New York: John Wiley.

Wildavsky, Aaron. 1964. *The politics of the budgetary process*. Boston: Little, Brown.

Wilson, Rick K. 1986. Forward and backward agenda procedures: Committee experiments on structurally induced equilibria. *Journal of Politics* 48:390–409.

INDEX

. . . . .

Agenda control: and congressional committees, 88–90; and covering relationship, 117; and equilibrium, 112; initially establishing, 87–88; and intransitive social preferences, 80–81; and multidimensional theories, 82–90; and stability, 114; as sufficient condition, 92; and unidimensional theories, 77–82

Agenda process, backward moving: and advantaging status quo, 97; affect on outcomes, 93–98; defined, 18–19, 93; and division of question rule, 103; and equilibrium, 93, 95, 96, 112, 114; in legislative theory, 127; as limitations on possible outcomes, 97–98; in literature, 94–95; in real legislatures, 94–95, 98; and reducing chaos, 96; and sophisticated agenda equilibrium, 117; and sophisticated voting, 104; and uncovered set, 123

Agenda process, endogenous: defined, 118; and sophisticated agenda equilibrium, 118; and uncovered set, 123

Agenda process, forward moving: defined, 93; effect on outcome, 93–98; and equilibrium, 94, 112; in legislatures, 94–95; in literature, 94–95; in Shepsle model, 102; and sophisticated agenda equilibrium, 117; and uncovered set, 122–23

Agricultural Appropriations Act, 28

Amendment level division of question, 102, 106

American Political Science Association, xi

American Political Science Review, xi

Anderson amendment, 29

Arrow, Kenneth, 27–28

Arrow paradox. *See* Paradox of voting

Bach, Stanley: and closed rules, 137; and congressional rules, 138; and germaneness rules, 106

Behavioral approach, xii

Bennett, William, 2

Birnbaum, Jeffrey, 67, 133

Black, Duncan, 138; and Condorcet, 134; logic of theorem, 23; and median outcomes, 37; and representation of preferences, 14–17; and sincere voting, 135; and single-peaked preferences, 14, 16; theorem, 17–20, 61, 62, 111–112; theorem in multiple dimensions, 60; use of theorem, 25

Blydenburgh, John, 30–31, 68

Bond, Jon, 137

Braybrook, David, 95

Brown v. *Board of Education*, 48

Buchanan, James, 133

Chaos theorems, 66–67

City block metric, 58, 59–60

The Logic of Lawmaking

Designed by Ann Walston

Composed by NK Graphics
in Times Roman with Helvetica Condensed display

Printed by The Maple Press Company
on 50-lb. MV Eggshell Cream